VENOMOUS
SNAKES

· WILD GUIDE ·

VENOMOUS SNAKES

Cynthia Berger

illustrations by Emily Damstra

STACKPOLE BOOKS

Published by
STACKPOLE BOOKS
5067 Ritter Road
Mechanicsburg, PA 17055
www.stackpolebooks.com

Printed in China

10 9 8 7 6 5 4 3 2 1

First edition

Cover design by Caroline Stover
Cover illustration by Emily Damstra
Illustrations by Emily Damstra
Photos by Dan Nedrelo and Allen Blake Sheldon

Library of Congress Cataloging-in-Publication Data

Berger, Cynthia.
    Venomous snakes / Cynthia Berger ; illustrations by Emily Damstra.
    — 1st ed.
        p.   cm. — (Wild guide)
    ISBN-13: 978-0-8117-3412-7
    ISBN-10: 0-8117-3412-9
    1. Poisonous snakes.   I. Title.

QL666.O6B444 2007
597.96'165—dc22

                                                              2007009564

CONTENTS

PREFACE

I'm a radio producer for a National Public Radio member station in rural Pennsylvania, and one of my regular projects is a series called "Pennsylvania Radio Expeditions." It's modeled after the famous "Radio Expeditions" program sponsored by the National Geographic Society and NPR. To produce that show, radio journalists traipse along with scientists to such exotic places as the Amazon or Antarctica, then create "audio postcards" of the fieldwork and the funky animal sounds.

My radio expeditions are more modest—one-day treks in Pennsylvania's wildlands with professors from our local universities. I do focus on our state's threatened species, and one species that's in trouble here is the timber rattlesnake. In the mid-twentieth century, hunters cleared out snakes by the hundreds from den sites all over the mountains, dragging them down to little towns for weekend festivals known as rattlesnake roundups. Snake populations have also declined as snake habitat has been altered or destroyed.

Last summer, I headed north and west from our home base in State College to a remote, wooded area where Rutgers University biology professor Howard Reinert has been studying timber rattlesnakes. One section of the study site was due to be logged, and Reinert wanted to see how the change in tree cover would affect the snake population.

Over the years, Reinert has fitted a number of snakes with radio transmitters so that he can track their movements over the course of the year. (Timber rattlesnakes make regular migrations between their winter den sites and summer feeding grounds.) He arranged for me to head out into the woods with his research assistant, Bill Monroe, to look for one of these snakes—snake number 143.

Fine-tuning the radio receiver, Bill led the way into the forest. We didn't follow any trail. He just figured out where the sound of the signal was strongest and walked in that general direction. The forest floor was completely covered with knee-high lime-green ferns, and our feet disappeared beneath them at every step.

Finally, after about half a mile of bushwhacking, Bill stopped. "There's our snake!" he announced. Using the tip of the metal antenna, he nudged a clump of ferns. There, coiled neatly at the base, was a slender lemon-yellow timber rattlesnake, gazing calmly up at us.

My friends always like to hear me tell stories about my adventures at work. But whenever I tell this story, the reaction is the same: horrified gasps. "You'd never catch me running around in the woods deliberately looking for rattlesnakes!" people say. "Weren't you terrified?"

Actually, no. We were wearing heavy leather boots and protective shin guards called snake chaps. We were beyond the snake's striking distance. We didn't touch the snake, and its calm behavior showed that it didn't feel threatened.

Fear of snakes is pervasive in our culture—and popular culture often perpetuates snakes' bad reputation. The 2006 movie *Snakes on a Plane* is the most recent case in point; it pretended to include in its script messages about tolerance for snakes and the need to protect and conserve them. But it was packed with misinformation.

Yet research shows that snakes play a key role in ecosystems. Young snakes are food for many predators. Adults snakes can be top predators, helping to control the populations of small rodents, lizards, and other snakes. Contrary to popular belief (and to the scenes in *Snakes on a Plane*), venomous snakes do not attack people; they bite only in self-defense. They would rather run away than fight.

My mother, Kitty Berger, has always been a friend to animals, and after retiring from her job as a public school teacher in Springfield, Massachusetts, she launched a program at the city's Forest Park Zoo called "Zoo on the Go" to bring animals into school classrooms, nursing homes, and similar venues for educational programs. She enjoyed showing off the screech-owl, the tarantula, and the lemur . . . but the snakes were always her favorites.

When mom would bring out Rosy the Boa, the kids in the audience would shriek with fear and lean back in their seats. Then she'd give them the straight talk about snakes. By the end of the hour she'd be coaxing them to touch the boa's warm, dry scales, maybe even draping Rosy around their necks. Lesson learned.

I hope this book can help people to appreciate snakes as much as Kitty Berger did.

INTRODUCTION

You're walking down a forest path at twilight when suddenly, out of the corner of your eye, you see a slim shape on the path in front of you. Instinctively—without even thinking—you jump back. A snake!

No, just a twig. But ophidiophobia, the irrational fear of snakes, is a very common human emotion. (Perhaps only spiders elicit an equally strong response.) One reason for this fear is cultural. In the Judeo-Christian tradition, snakes are a symbol of evil. The serpent tempts Eve with forbidden knowledge in the Garden of Eden. The New Testament alludes to a connection between snakes and Satan. Revelation 12:9, for example, talks about "that ancient serpent called the devil, or Satan."

Fear of snakes seems to go well beyond what we've learned in religious school, however. A recent study by one Swedish psychologist concluded that the fear of snakes is so deep-rooted, it's probably instinctive. It may have originated with the very first mammals, two hundred million years ago, living in a world dominated by reptiles. Fear of snakes passed down from those tiny, shrewlike creatures to all of their descendents—including us.

From an evolutionary perspective, this conclusion makes some sense. Fear of venomous snakes would be an adaptive response in nature, since individuals with a strong fear response would be more likely to avoid venomous snakes, survive, and have offspring—who would then pass on the instinct.

Recently, anthropology professor Lynne Isabell of the University of California, Davis, put forward some additional support for this idea. She contends that the ability to spot venomous snakes seems to have played a key role in the evolution of sharp vision and other traits in monkeys, apes, and humans.

As you probably know, many primates have excellent eyesight, big brains, and very dexterous hands and feet. Formerly, scientists thought these traits evolved as primates fine-tuned their ability to catch small insect prey or pick fruit from trees. But according to Isabell, the need to spot and avoid venomous snakes may have been the driving evolutionary force.

As evidence, Isabell looked to the joint history of snakes and primates. She found that the species of monkeys with the sharpest eyesight were the ones who lived in closest proximity to venomous snakes for the greatest length of time.

The story goes like this. About sixty million years ago, primates separated into two groups: the Old World monkeys and apes, and the lemurs of Madagascar. Snakes had been around on Earth for a while, but around the same time the primates made their split, the first venomous snakes appeared on the scene. They showed up in Africa and Asia, the same continents as some of the Old World monkeys.

About thirty-five million years ago, the Old World monkeys split again, and some groups colonized South America. But venomous snakes didn't arrive in South America until millions of years later. So monkeys were living in South America for quite a while without having to deal with any venomous snakes.

Old World monkeys, which have coexisted for the longest with venomous snakes, have the sharpest vision and the best color vision. New World monkeys have less specialized vision—and they react with less fear to snakes. Lemurs, which have no venomous snakes in their environment, have visual powers basically unchanged over the past sixty million years . . . and they have no fear of snakes at all.

That's all very suggestive. But there's also physical evidence, says Isabell. Neurological studies show that, in an Old World monkey's brain, the visual system seems to be connected to structures involved in vigilance, fear, and learning—*not* to structures used for reaching and grasping.

Given that fear of snakes seems to be an instinctive reaction for a primate, perhaps you're saying, well, then, it's reasonable for me to be afraid of venomous snakes, too. But herpetologists, biologists who study snakes, say that even if fear of snakes has an instinctive component, this fear is unreasonably amplified through misinformation and ignorance. With correct information about snake behavior, you can enjoy the out-of-doors safely, and appreciate these fascinating animals from a respectful distance.

The U.S. Centers for Disease Control, which keeps track of these things, finds that most bites from venomous snakes in America are to the hands, suggesting the snake had been handled, not accidentally stepped on. Most snakebite victims are young males. Often, alcohol is involved.

Popular culture persists in maligning snakes. The movie *Snakes on a Plane* was just the latest in a long line of Hollywood films to present a boatload, or planeload, of misinformation about venomous snakes.

Legend has it that the movie's title was the entire "pitch." What could be scarier than being trapped in a small space with a bunch of venomous snakes?

Screenwriter David Dalessandro did base the movie on a real-life incident. Apparently this University of Pittsburgh college administrator read an article in a nature magazine about brown tree snakes on the island nation of Guam slithering onto planes and hitchhiking their way to Hawaii. This actually happened.

Not much else in the movie was realistic, however. In case you missed it, the plot involved a witness to a gang murder in Hawaii who is flown to Los Angles to testify in the trial. The gang leader doesn't want the witness to arrive alive, so he secretly loads crates of venomous snakes on the plane; the crates have time-release doors that open midway through the flight. Meanwhile, passengers boarding the flight get draped with flower necklaces that have been secretly sprayed with snake pheromones to make the stowaway snakes aggressive. Released from their crates, the snakes swarm the plane and attack the passengers, biting them in creative places.

Plenty of people—including the librarian who checked out my snake reference books at the Penn State University library—refused to see this movie because it touched their deep-rooted fears. Yet almost nothing depicted in this movie could really happen.

For example, the snakes are transported in the cargo hold, which is quite cold. Real snakes would have become sluggish and unlikely to leave the crates in a cold environment.

Assuming they did crawl out, snakes prefer enclosed spaces to bright lights and open spaces. They'd be far more likely to disappear into dark corners than to come racing down the aisles of the plane.

Chasing the passengers is completely unrealistic behavior. Any venomous snake you might encounter in North America would prefer not to interact with you. If it saw you, its first line of action would be to freeze and hope you wouldn't notice it. Next, it might try to run away. Only if it couldn't find a hiding place and felt you were an imminent threat might it try to strike at you.

The movie explains the aggressive behavior by the snake pheromones sprayed on the flower necklaces. However, female snakes are the ones that release pheromones, to signal they are ready to mate. So male snakes would be attracted with amorous, not aggressive, intentions. And each snake would only be drawn to the pheromones of its own species.

Finally, two-thirds of the snakes you see in the move are not even real; they're computer generated or animatronic. And virtually all of the snakes in the movie are, in fact, nonvenomous—except for two individuals, a cobra and an eastern diamondback rattlesnake.

How much should you worry about being bitten by a real, live venomous snake in North America? Let's put it in perspective. According to the U.S. Centers for Disease Control, each year in the United States about eight hundred thousand people are seriously bitten by domestic dogs. In the same year, about seven thousand people per year are bitten by venomous snakes—and those bites result, on average, in about five deaths per year—half the number of deaths due to dog attacks.

Of those seven thousand snakebites, many could be avoided by a little common sense. Half or more are the result of someone trying to pick up or kill the snake. According to national studies, ninety-five percent of all bites are on an extremity; fifty-six percent are on the hand, which mean they're not the result of stepping on a snake accidentally. White males account for three-quarters of all victims; half are young, between the ages of eighteen to twenty-eight. Often, alcohol is involved; medical professionals report that forty to a hundred percent of venomous snakebite victims they treat are drunk.

Furthermore, the snakes themselves are reluctant attackers. They know you are not prey, and they don't really want to waste their precious venom on you; after all, a venomless bite will do as good a job of scaring you away as a bite loaded with venom. The data show that about one-fourth of the time, when venomous snakes strike a person, they inject no venom at all. With most other bites, the snake injects only a small amount of venom.

If you're worried about violence in nature, watch out for bad weather: you have a one in two million annual risk of being killed by a tornado. Be wary of seismic phenomena: you have a one in eleven million chance of being killed in an earthquake or volcanic eruption. Don't take a chance on technology either; you have a one in twenty-five million chance of being hit by a falling airplane, and if you drive ten thousand miles a year, your risk of dying in a traffic accident is about one in six thousand.

Your risk of dying from the bite of a venomous snake, however, is just one in thirty-six million. You're far more likely to be struck by lightning, succumb to bubonic plague, be struck by salmonella poisoning, get snuffed out in a house fire, die by choking, or slip and fall and kill yourself in the bathtub than you are to be killed by a venomous snake.

Venomous snakes are not at all common in North America. Most states are home to just a few species, and you are not likely to see them unless you know where to look. Venomous snakes make up a small minority of the snakes you might ever encounter. Worldwide, there are about 3,000 species of snakes; of these, about 515 species are venomous, and of the venomous species, only a small number are considered a serious risk to humans.

The United States is home to about 115 species of snakes; of these, 20 species are venomous. This book will help you learn about those species—how they live, catch prey, maintain a comfortable temperature, avoid danger, and find mates and perpetuate their own kind. A mini field guide offers identification tips and life history information for the nineteen land-dwelling species.

The venomous snakes of North American include two kinds of coral snakes, one sea snake, and seventeen kinds of pit vipers—the cottonmouth and copperhead (which are closely related to one another)—plus fifteen kinds of rattlesnakes.

Among the rattlesnakes, many of the species comprise a variety of subspecies, and each subspecies can be distinguished by uniquely beautiful and intricate scale patterns that matches their desert, forest, or grassland habitats. It's beyond the scope of this book to show all the different subspecies; for each species, the most common subspecies is depicted.

Venomous snakes may loom large in our consciousness, but in reality some are surprisingly tiny. Coral snakes are no thicker than a pencil. A coiled baby dusky pygmy rattlesnake fits neatly on a quarter. On the other end of the scale, there's the massive eastern diamondback. The largest specimens can be thicker through the body than a man's leg, measure as much as eight feet long, and weigh up to fifty pounds. It's the heaviest venomous snake on the planet.

Many of North America's venomous snake species are declining in numbers due to years of bounty hunting and loss of habitat, so this book also includes a section on conservation issues. And because snakes figure so prominently in religion and literature around the world, there's a chapter on venomous snakes in folklore and mythology. The Bible may connect snakes with the devil, but not all traditions put snakes in this light. Some cultures see them as a symbol of rebirth and immortality. Others regard them as one of the wisest of animals.

1

What Makes a Snake?

At first glance, a snake seems like simple animal, not much more than a length of inner tube. Superficially, it seems to have the same body plan as some lower life forms, such as earthworms, tubeworms, roundworms, and planaria. It has no limbs—no arms or legs or wings or fins or flippers. It has no obvious protuberances to help it sense or interact with its environment— no feelers or antennae or whiskers.

Yet despite such apparent simplicity, snakes are complex. They have far more in common with you and me than with the lowly worms they resemble.

Taxonomically speaking, snakes are members of the phylum Chordata, a group that includes animals with backbones. Taxonomists subdivide this group into a number of smaller categories, or classes. Snakes are in the class Reptilia—the reptiles.

Reptiles are a diverse bunch. Lizards, turtles, crocodiles, and alligators are all reptiles; but the category also includes some obscure lizardlike critters called tuataras, found only in New Zealand, plus the truly oddball amphisbaenians—the legless, burrowing "worm lizards" of Africa and South America.

What Makes a Reptile?

One trait that reptiles share is skin covered with hard, protective scales. Another shared trait is that they use lungs to breathe. And all reptiles have a three-chambered heart—simpler in structure than the human heart, which has four chambers.

Also, all reptiles are ectothermic, which means they're unable to generate their own body heat through metabolic means, the way mammals and birds do. Some people call reptiles "cold-blooded" instead of ectothermic, but this is a bit of a misnomer; it suggests that a reptile's blood is always cold, and it most definitely is not. Reptiles rely on the outside environment as a thermal source, and they keep their body temperature within an optimal range through their behavior. They seek out warm places when they need to warm up and cool places when they need to cool off.

As for reproductive strategies, some reptiles lay hard-shelled eggs, the way birds do. Others give birth to live young. In either case, the mother generally doesn't do much to care for her offspring.

Taxonomists divide the class Reptilia into three subclasses: one for alligators and crocodiles, which have a distinctively shaped skull; one for turtles, which are unique in having a body covered in very hard, bony plates; and one for snakes, lizards, tuataras, and amphisbaenians. These last four groups get put together in a single subclass called Ledpidosauria because all have scales that overlap one another.

So what makes snakes unique? At the next taxonomic level, the tuatara, which has a distinctive kind of skull, gets its own order, Sphenodontia. But snakes are still grouped with lizards and amphisbaenians in the order Squamata, based on similarities in the shape of *their* skulls.

It's at the level of the suborder that taxonomists split snakes from the other groups. Lizards are in the suborder Sauria (the Greek root word in *dinosaur*). Amphisbaenians have their own suborder, Amphisbaenia (let's just say, they're really weird). And snakes are in the suborder Serpentes.

Look Ma, No Legs

So, what makes a snake? One obvious difference between lizards and snakes is that lizards have legs and snakes do not. Also, compared to lizards, snakes have unusually elongated bodies. Here, we have to qualify the statement. A few lizard species have evolved to a legless state. And a few members of some snake groups, including the boas and pythons, have vestigial hind legs. But these vestigial legs are so tiny that, if you're not a snake biologist and don't know exactly where to look, chances are you would never notice them. They look more like tiny spurs than legs. None of the venomous snakes mentioned in this book has vestigial legs.

Furthermore, no snake has shoulder bones, and only the most primitive snakes have small vestiges of pelvic bones. Even legless lizards have these bones.

Flexibility

Another thing that makes snakes unique among reptiles is that they have no sternum. Also known as the breastbone, the sternum is the long, flat bone that runs down the center of the chest. In most vertebrates, the sternum is the

Meals go down headfirst . . . always swallowed whole. This eastern massasauga is engulfing a cottontail rabbit with a body diameter much larger than its own. It can accomplish this feat thanks to its highly flexible jaws. Rings of cartilage keep its trachea open, so it can breathe while swallowing. Using its teeth—first on one side of the mouth, then the other—it can ratchet the meal down; it also uses its fangs to manipulate the meal. Swallowing a big meal like this can take up to an hour.

structure to which the ends of the ribs are anchored by cartilage; the result is rigid yet flexible cage that protects the heart.

Because the snake's ribs are not attached at the ends, its heart is a little less protected; on the other hand, the free-floating ribs give the snake an advantage when it comes to swallowing its prey whole (which is what snakes do)—the ribs can expand greatly, allowing the big bolus of food to slide on down.

Another trait that separates snakes from lizards is their unusually flexible jaw mechanism. The bones that make up a snake's jaws are attached to one another fairly loosely so that the entire unit can stretch, much like a beaded bracelet strung on elastic cord. This means a snake can open very, very wide and swallow animals larger in diameter than its own body.

That might seem like it would put a strain on the internal organs through which the meal must pass, such as the esophagus (or gullet) and the stomach. But these structures, too, are highly elastic.

The Guts

Because of their tube-steak body plan, snakes have unusually elongated internal organs. Certain organs always come in pairs: two lungs, two kidneys, two ovaries, two testes. In most animals, these organs are arranged in the body side by side, so that if the body were split in half down the long axis, the two sides would make mirror images of one another.

In snakes, however, the paired organs are arranged in the body in staggered positions—one is stationed further down the body than the other. The organs also tend to be long and thin, almost cigar shaped. The lungs take this modification even farther. In most snakes, there's only one long, thin right lung; the left lung either is very small and doesn't function, or is absent.

As for how snakes get air into that lung, they lack the muscular membrane below the lungs, called the diaphragm, which all mammals have. Snakes inflate their lungs another way, by expanding their flexible rib cages, much the way you might pump a bellows. If you watch a quietly resting snake, this movement is quite obvious.

Although snakes have two kidneys, they have no urinary bladder. Their urine drains directly to an opening called a cloaca. The cloaca is a multipurpose opening—it's also the outlet for wastes from the intestinal tract and, whether the snake is a male or female, the outlet for the genital tract. Snakes that lay eggs push them out through the cloaca, and snakes that give birth to live young do so through the cloaca. The location of the cloaca marks the point at which the snake's body is considered to end and its tail begins.

Snake Sex

When it comes to reproduction, snakes are like other vertebrates: male snakes have testes and female snakes have ovaries. What makes snakes distinctive is how males are equipped to have sex: they have two copulatory organs called hemipenes (if you are referring to just one, it's a hemipenis.)

The hemipenes look like a single organ—short and stubby and forked at the tip. They tend to have complicated ornaments in the form of short spikes or spines. The shape of the hemipenes are very distinctive for each species of snake; in fact, taxonomists use the shape and ornamentation of the hemipenes as a definitive way to identify snakes to species (of course, that's not very useful for the average person looking at snakes in the wild).

Most of the time, the hemipenes are tucked away, inside out, inside the snake's body, in a pocket behind the cloaca. This is why a male snake often seems to have a longer, thicker tail than a female. When the snake is ready to mate, blood inflates the hemipenes and they evert to stick out through his cloaca.

In order to fertilize a female snake's eggs, the male inserts one or the other half of the hemipenes into the female's cloaca. The spines or hooks latch onto the walls of her cloaca. When the two snakes mate, they stay hooked together for hours. The hemipenes has a deep groove down the length of its outer surface and the sperm flows down this groove into the female's cloaca. (In some snake species, the females can store this sperm for months or even years, and the sperm will stay viable until the eggs are finally fertilized.) When mating is complete, the male uses a special retractor muscle to disengage his hemipenes from the female's cloaca.

The Forked Tongue

One snake trait that many people seem to find sinister is the forked tongue, which is another trait that generally distinguishes snakes from lizards; only one group of lizards has evolved this characteristic.

Watch a snake for any length of time and you'll notice that it flicks its forked tongue repeatedly—sticking it out, drawing it back into its mouth. What's going on? Tongue-flicking is how the snake smells its way to food, a mate, or a den site. Each time the snake sticks its tongue out, odor molecules stick to the damp surface. The snake pulls its tongue back into its mouth and inserts it into a special place in the nasal cavity where it has a sensory organ called the Jacobson's organ. The organ processes the molecules, and the snake orients to its target.

Why is that tongue forked? It's not merely to give the snake a diabolical look. Researchers now think the forked tongue is the smell equivalent of binocular vision. It seems that when the snake sticks its tongue out, it also spreads the two forks wide. Biologists think the snake may be collecting molecules from two separate points in the air. By collecting data from two points along a gradient, the snake may be able to tell where the smell is stronger, and where it is weaker, and better orient in the right direction.

All snakes have a Jacobson's organ they can use to smell their way to food and mates. Rattlesnakes are unique among North American snakes for the heat-sensitive organs on their heads called loreal pits. (This is why they are called pit vipers.) Each snake has two pits, located between the eyes and nostrils. They rather look like a second set of nostrils.

The pits can detect infrared radiation. Even in complete dark, a rattlesnake can sense the heat given off by a creature as small as a mouse against the background of the cooler night air.

Scales

Many people assume snakes are slimy, but just touch one and see. The scales are dry and tough; they're made from a material similar to fingernails.

Superficially, a snake's scales may look like fish scales, in that they are oval and overlapping. But a fish's scales are loose and separate, lightly attached to the skin. A snake's scales *are* its skin—they're a layer of dead cells. They will not grow with the snake. So in order for the snake to grow bigger, it must shed or slough off this hard outer covering. A new layer of skin is waiting underneath. Snakes shed their skin all in one piece, at least once a year and sometimes more often.

To protect their eyes from wind and dust, snakes have built-in goggles. Each eye is covered by a single transparent scale, called a brille. This scale is part of the skin, so that when the snake sheds, it also sheds the eye covering and gets an unscratched new one. (Snakes need these goggles because they can't blink—they have no eyelids. That's another thing that sets them apart from most other reptiles, although a few species of lizards also lack eyelids.)

Some snakes have scales that are keeled, which means each scale has a little ridge running right down the middle, giving the snake a rough appearance. Other snakes have smooth, unkeeled scales. All rattlesnakes have keeled scales; a number of nonvenomous rattlesnake look-alikes could easily be mistaken for these species, but have unkeeled scales (along with other distinguishing traits). The arrangement and number of scales on a snake's head can be a clue as to whether or not it is a venomous snake. And the number of scales widthwise, across a snake's back, from belly scale to belly scale, can also be a key to its identity (because scales are arranged on a diagonal, you have to count in a V formation).

No Ears, Still Can Hear

Although lizards don't have pinna, or ear flaps, the way humans and mammals do, most lizards do have external ear openings—holes you can see on the sides of the head. Snakes, in contrast, have no external ear openings, and for this reason, many people assume snakes are deaf.

Snakes can, in fact, hear, but they hear in a slightly different way than humans do. They lack the various complicated parts of the ear that make up our middle ear—no ear drum, eustachian tube, or multiple ossicles to transmit sound waves.

Instead, all that snakes have for a hearing apparatus is a single small bone called the columella on each side of the head. The columella connects the quadrate bone (in the jaw) to the inner ear canals. Snakes use this system to pick up sound in three dimensions. They use their skin rather than an ear opening as the sound-wave receptor, to pick up sounds from both the air and the ground (some evidence suggests that the snake's single lung also acts as a sound receptor).

Size and arrangement of head scales help you distinguish between the two groups of rattlesnakes. Members of the genus Crotalus, such as this eastern diamondback (Crotalus adamanteus), have heads completely covered in small scales that are all pretty much the same shape. Members of the genus Sistrurus, in contrast, have a conspicuous cluster of nine very large scales on the head. The cluster starts near the nose and is arranged in rows of two, two, three, and then two scales.

A PIT VIPER'S SECRET WEAPON

New research from Germany shows that pit vipers—which mostly sense their environment using the heat detectors in their facial pits, not their eyes—seem to have a similar ability built into their brains.

To understand this process, think back to when you were a kid. Did you ever use a pinhole camera, a primitive camera without a lens? The tiny hole, no bigger than a pinprick, focuses the light that enters the camera onto one tiny point, which produces a crisp image.

Scientists have known for a long time that a pit viper's pit organs work much like a pinhole camera. The main difference is that instead of admitting visible light waves, each pit takes in infrared light (heat). And instead of the film inside a camera, each pit has a membrane stretched across it that's capable of detecting infrared light.

But compared to the pinhole of a pinhole camera, a pit organ is pretty large—about as big across as a pencil eraser. That means a snake must be getting a blurry image from these detectors. If the hole at the top of the pit were small enough to produce a crisp image, it would be too small to let in enough infrared waves to stimulate the membrane.

Using computer modeling, physicists at the Technical University of Munich concluded that some snakes probably use a simple network of neurons in their brains to correct the image. An infrared signal from each of the membrane's heat receptors triggers a neuron to fire. The firing rate varies with respect to input from the other receptors. There are about two thousand heat receptors in a single pit; it seems that the brain's network of neurons can process how the receptors interact, and sharpen up the image accordingly. The end result? A snake sinks its fangs into its warm, furry target.

Snakes hear low-frequency sounds best—around 200 to 500 Hz, which is at the lower end of human hearing. As they lie in wait for prey, they can pick up the most subtle vibrations from its movements . . . transmitted through sand, leaf litter, dried grass, and even hard ground.

Evolutionary History

Around the world, scientists have identified about 2,700 different species of snakes, grouped into 11 different families. The majority of the world's snakes are members of the Colubrid family, a diverse group that includes such familiar species as rat snakes, garter snakes, king snakes, and hognose snakes.

Here in North America, you can find about 115 different species of snakes from 5 different families. Three of the families are considered nonvenomous snakes. Besides colubrids, we have snakes in the Slender Blind Snake family—tiny, burrowing snakes that look more like earthworms—and snakes in the Boa and Python family, such as the rosy boa and rubber boa, found in the western United States.

Black nose, yellow ring—that's a distinguishing field mark for the coral snake. Compare this member of the Elapid family to the eastern diamondback, a member of the Viper family, and notice some other distinguishing traits: the very smooth scales, the head that's not much wider than the body, and the round pupils.

A QUICK GUIDE

FAMILY ELAPIDAE (the coral snakes, kraits, and mambas)
- Includes snakes with fangs at the front of the mouth
- These fangs do not fold up; instead they fit into a pocket in the gums when not in use
- Pupils of the eyes are round
- Body scales are very smooth
- Venom is neurotoxic; affects heart function and breathing but causes little or no damage at the bite site

Present in North America:

Subfamily Micrurinae

Genus *Micrurus* and *Micruroides* (coral snakes)
- Famous for their alternating bands of bright colors

Subfamily Hydrophiinae

Genus *Pelamis* (sea snake)
- Nostrils have valves that form a seal when the snake dives
- The body scales do not overlap
- Tail is flattened vertically into a paddle

FAMILY VIPERIDAE (the vipers)
- Includes snakes with hollow fangs at the front of the mouth
- These fangs fold up when not in use
- The pupils of the eye are vertical (elliptical)
- Body scales are keeled (ridged) so the snake has a rough appearance
- Venom is mostly hemotoxic; causes severe damage at the bite site, including tissue death

Subfamily Crotalinidae (the pit vipers)
- Noted for their "pits," special heat-sensing organs, located on the head between the eye and nostril

Present in North America:

Genus *Agkistrodon:* the copperhead and the cottonmouth

Genus *Crotalus* and *Sistrurus:* the rattlesnakes (fifteen species)

The other two families represented in North America are the venomous snakes: the elapids (represented here by coral snakes and sea snakes) and the vipers (represented here by cottonmouths, copperheads, and rattlesnakes). All of these snakes make venom in modified salivary glands and inject it into their prey using two fangs located at the front of the mouth (for more about venom, see chapter 2).

How could a reptile that injects poison through its teeth have evolved? Scientists have been studying the evolutionary history of venomous snakes, trying to understand their family tree. For years, researchers held one idea about the lines of descent. But in just the past few years, new evidence has turned up, suggesting that a complete overhaul of the snake family tree is called for.

Here's what scientists know. Lizards first show up in the fossil record in the Triassic Period, which was 248 to 206 million years ago. Snakes don't make very good fossils—their bones are very delicate, so they're rarely preserved—but from the few records that exist, it seems the first snakes showed up later on, in the Jurassic Period (206 to 144 million years ago). Snakes are thought to be the direct descendents of lizards: after all, they are basically elongated, legless lizards.

Of the various snake families that exist worldwide, the one with the most species and the most individuals is the colubrids. The majority of the snakes in this group are not venomous.

As noted above, the two families of venomous snakes found in North America are the vipers and the elapids. Formerly, scientists believed that all vipers (including rattlesnakes) and elapids (including coral snakes and the yellow-bellied sea snake) had evolved from the colubrids. The first true venomous snakes were thought to have showed up on the scene about a hundred million years ago. The fact that snakes are descended from lizards wasn't thought to be a very important factor in the evolution of venomous snakes, given that just two lizard species were thought to be venomous, the Gila monster and the Mexican beaded lizard. Scientists figured those two lizard species had evolved their venom-producing powers completely independently of snakes.

Now, lots of people keep lizards as pets, so people knew that if you get bitten by a lizard, very often you'd have a pretty bad reaction, with lots of swelling and bleeding. But everyone figured that lizards chew on some pretty nasty stuff, so lizard bites are likely to get infected.

Then herpetologists took a more careful look. They determined that those bad bites were the result of lizard venom. It turns out that far more lizards actually have a venomous bite than anyone imagined.

Not only that, but herpetologists also tested saliva from a number of snakes that were considered to be nonvenomous, such as the common rat snake. They discovered that this species (and many others) actually have venom components in their saliva.

At the same time, taxonomists were using a new tool to look at relationships among species. Rather than looking just at visible features—the shape of bones or teeth or the hemipenes—they looked directly at DNA, the genetic code of each species.

What they determined is that venomous lizards and venomous snakes did not evolve their ability to make venom separately. They share a common ancestor: a lizardlike creature that lived about two hundred million years ago. This finding pushes back the date for the evolution of venomous reptiles by about a hundred million years.

Now, two hundred million years before the present is roughly the time when the first small mammals started running around on Earth. So some biologists speculate venom systems evolved as lizards and snakes started to take advantage of this new source of food.

2

All About Venom

When you're talking about coral snakes and rattlesnakes, do you call them "poisonous snakes"? It's a common thing to do, but strictly speaking, it's a semantic mistake. Scientists like to be precise, and they're especially precise about the meaning of words. Coral snakes and rattlesnakes are *venomous*, not poisonous.

Dig into the etymological history of the word venom, and you'll find it came into general usage around the thirteenth century in France. The modern English word "venom" is derived from the Latin word *venenum,* meaning "a poison, drug, or potion." Scholars speculate that venenum could also refer to Venus, the goddess of erotic love (in that case, the "potion" part of the definition would refer a love potion, which might be sweet or deadly).

The ancient definition still applies today. When we say "venom" we mean "a kind of poison." But in scientific terms, venom is a very specific kind of poison. By definition, a poison is "anything that can cause illness, injury, or death to a living creature." But we're talking injury or death in a particular way—not through physical means such as crushing, cutting, or suffocation, but injury through chemistry. A poison is something that causes injury through a chemical reaction or molecular activity.

The definition of a poison covers a lot of ground. As you probably know, many elements and compounds can be useful and even essential to your health in small amounts, yet poisonous in excessive amounts. Salt is one example; zinc is another. Other compounds, such as arsenic, are just poisonous, though a low dosage may cause illness rather than death.

Venoms fall into a subcategory of poisons called toxins. Toxins are poisons that are made by living creatures. Poison-dart frogs ooze toxins from pores in their backs. The irritating sap of poison ivy is a toxin. Botox, the compound that women use voluntarily to paralyze their facial muscles and erase wrinkles, is, as its name so clearly shows, a toxin; it's produced by the bacterium *Clostridium botulinum*. If you were to swallow the *botulinum* toxin, you'd be sick to your stomach with food poisoning.

The heavy metals mercury, lead, and selenium are examples of materials that can poison you but are not toxins. All of these are elements. They are found in nature, but they are not produced by living creatures.

So venoms are toxins—compounds produced by living creatures—but they fall into another particular subcategory. Venoms are toxins that are delivered through a bite or a sting or some other device that resembles a hypodermic needle. If the poison gets jabbed into the victim through a fang or a stinger, it's a venom.

Literary clichés pick up on this scientific distinction. Writers often say a character's language is "venomous" when they want to convey the notion of very sharp and stinging words.

Who Packs Venom?

Snakes are probably the best-known venomous animals. But many other animals do use venom. Animals use venom for two main reasons: protection from predators and to hunt for food. Some animals use their venom for both reasons.

The main reason snakes use venom is to immobilize their prey, which makes it easier to swallow. Defensive action is a side benefit for snakes.

Another side benefit for snakes is that venom acts like meat tenderizer and begins the digestive process. This is very handy when you are swallowing your meal whole instead of biting and chewing.

You can find venomous animals almost everywhere: on land, in freshwater ecosystems, in the ocean, deserts, forests, jungles, and lowlands. Every major animal group—with the exception of birds—includes a species or two that is venomous (and some ornithologists assert that there's one bird with venomous feathers, the hooded pitohui of New Guinea). Besides snakes, some of the most commonplace venomous animals include bees and spiders.

Instead of delivering venom by biting, bees use a stinger. This structure, located on the tip of the abdomen, evolved from the ovipositor, or egg-laying apparatus. For the familiar honeybee, stinging is the ultimate act of self-sacrifice—when it stings, the stinger rips out of its body and stays in the victim, and the bee dies. It's all for the collective good of the hive. Other bees and bee relatives, such as wasps and hornets, have a different body design and can sting repeatedly. (It's important to note that not all bees sting. In fact, quite a number of native North American bees do not sting—but they get a bad rep because of their stinging relations.)

With venomous spiders, as with venomous snakes, the danger is generally from the bite. In North America, spiders that use venom to immobilize their prey include several species of black widows, brown spiders, and the brown recluse, along with the funnel-web spider. North American tarantulas are also venomous, but it's not that they bite—they have venomous body hairs as a defense mechanism.

Other notable venomous animals include scorpions, which deliver venom through stingers on their tails; tropical fish, including the scorpionfish, stonefish, and surgeonfish, which have venom glands at the base of some spines that support their fins; and lizards, including the Gila monster and beaded lizard in North America, which deliver venom through grooves in their teeth.

Even a few mammals are venomous. The male duck-billed platypus has venomous spurs on its ankles, thought to be an offensive weapon against other males, used during the breeding season. And several species of shrews have a venomous bite; these tiny mouselike hunters use their toxic saliva to paralyze their prey.

A Complex Compound

In contrast to bees with their stingers and platypuses with their spurs, all snakes deliver their venom through their bite. Snake venom is a thick and sticky liquid, generally yellowish in color, anywhere from deep amber to pale straw yellow. In very young snakes, venom is almost colorless. It's made inside a pair of modified salivary glands located at the rear of the upper jaw.

In coral snakes, a duct from each gland leads to the base of a grooved tooth; when the snake bites, the venom flows down the groove and into the victim. In vipers, the duct carries venom from the gland to the center of a hollow fang. The fang is slender and sharp, like a hypodermic needle, and like a needle it has a tiny hole near the sharp tip. By contracting muscles around each venom gland, the snake can control the amount of venom delivered by each of its two fangs.

At the molecular level, venom is very complex. It's made up largely of proteins, most of which are enzymes, large molecules that promote chemical reactions. Researchers have identified about twenty-five different enzymes in snake venoms collectively. Each species of venomous snake will have about seven to ten of these enzymes in its venom, along with other proteins, peptides, carbohydrates, and metals.

The enzymes are what make the venom so dangerous. The venoms of different snakes can be sorted into two very broad categories: those that are mostly hemotoxic and those that are mostly neurotoxic.

Enzymes that are hemotoxins attack the circulatory system by preventing blood from clotting or by breaking down blood and/or body tissue. Just how toxic such venom is varies from species to species. If you're bitten by a species with mostly hemotoxic venom, you may end up with a crater-shaped pockmark at the bite site due to tissue death; you may lose the entire limb that was bitten; or you may die from the bite. Eastern diamondback rattlesnakes have very potent hemotoxic venom. Copperhead venom is also hemotoxic, but not so dangerous.

Enzymes that are neurotoxins attack the nervous system. Neurotoxins can impair the senses and cause problems with breathing, or heart failure. When a snake with neurotoxic venom strikes its prey, the animal usually dies because it can't breathe.

This classification of venom enzymes into two categories is a bit of an oversimplification; most venoms actually have a mixture of properties. But it's a useful starting point for understanding the properties of venoms.

Venom is made in glands that had their evolutionary origin as salivary glands, and as it turns out, for the snakes themselves, the main purpose of venom is as an aid to digestion. After the snake strikes a prey animal, its circulatory system spreads the venom throughout its body, and the venom enzymes start the work of digestion from the inside out—even as the snake is starting to swallow its meal. This is helpful because the prey is swallowed whole, not cut up or broken apart or chewed in any way.

Each species of snake secretes its own unique venom, which is why if you do get bitten, it's so important to know what species bit you: you want to be treated (as quickly as possible) with the right kind of antivenin.

Antivenin is the antidote to a venomous snakebite. It neutralizes the venom circulating in your body. Antivenin cannot, however, reverse or undo any damage that venom may have already done to nerves or blood or tissue. That's why it's important to be treated quickly.

In order to make antivenin to treat bites from North America's venomous snakes, drug manufacturers currently rely on the immune systems of horses and sheep. The manufacturing process works like this: An animal is injected with a small (nonfatal) dose of snake venom. Its body responds by making antibodies (defensive proteins) against the venom. Antibodies do their work by attaching to venom molecules like signal tags, telling the body's immune system to "destroy this molecule."

From a few weeks to a year after the animal has been injected with venom, its blood is loaded with antibodies. In a process much like human blood donation, some of the blood is collected. First the red and white cells are removed, leaving the watery serum. Then the antibodies are purified from the serum to make antivenin.

Horse serum antivenin has been available in the United States since 1954. Although it has saved lives, the treatment can be worse than the ailment if the victim is allergic to horses. About a quarter of all patients treated with horse serum antivenin have some degree of allergic reaction to the serum, and some have died due to an extreme allergic reaction called anaphylactic shock.

Antivenin made using sheep instead of horses is a newer innovation. The trademarked product called CroFab has been treated in a way that reduces the

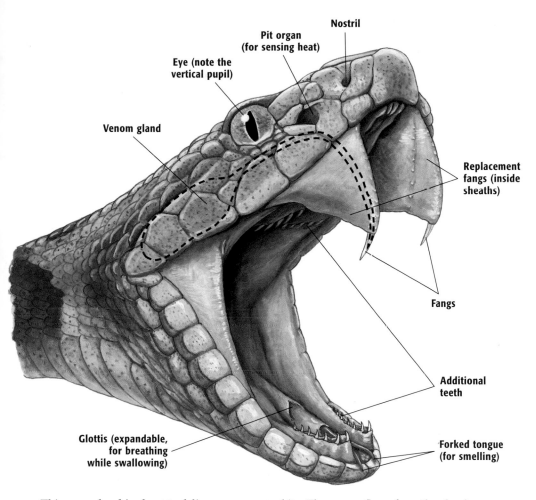

Nostril

Pit organ
(for sensing heat)

Eye (note the
vertical pupil)

Venom gland

Replacement
fangs (inside
sheaths)

Fangs

Additional
teeth

Glottis (expandable,
for breathing
while swallowing)

Forked tongue
(for smelling)

This copperhead is about to deliver a venomous bite. The venom flows from the glands in its cheeks through narrow ducts into the hollow fangs. Snakes can control how much venom they inject into prey using muscles that surround the glands.

risk of an allergic reaction. However, this antivenin is cleared from the body by the kidneys more rapidly than horse antivenin, so it may have to be administered again to treat a snakebite. That makes it more expensive.

Researchers continue to look for safer and more effective kinds of antivenin. One team based at the Liverpool School of Tropical Medicine in England has had preliminary success making antivenins by injecting animals with snake DNA rather than venom. They worked with the saw-scaled viper, a deadly African species. First, they isolated the genes that coded for certain components of the venom, including the enzymes that break down the lining of

WHAT IF YOU'RE BITTEN?

First of all, forget the snakebite remedies you learned about in Hollywood movies. Do not cut the wound and suck out the poison. Do not apply a tight tourniquet. Do not apply ice. Do not apply an electric shock. Do not have the patient drink alcohol.

The most effective snakebite kit is a car, a set of keys, and a cell phone. Stay calm, and get the victim to a hospital as quickly as possible.

It is helpful if you can identify what species of snake did the biting. But it's not essential. The antivenin formulations in America today are cocktails of the most common venomous snakes in the region, to cover all bases. There's no point wasting time rummaging through the shrubbery to hunt down and kill the snake while the victim urgently needs medical attention. You run the risk that yet another person will be bitten.

Keep the patient calm. The likelihood of dying is very low.

Bright red and bright yellow are nature's warning signs. They say, "Danger! Stay away!" The coral snake uses these colors to signal that it is venomous; this Nelson's milksnake is one of many "coral snake mimics" that also sends a scary message . . . even though its bite is harmless. Remember the rhyme: "Red touch yellow, kill a fellow. Red touch black, venom lack."

If venomous snakes are part of your local fauna, sensible precautions will reduce the risk of a dangerous encounter in the wild.

- Don't go hiking (or biking/or paddling) in the woods alone.
- Wear protective footgear and leg coverings. That means leather boots, not sandals, on the trail. For the most part, loose-fitting long pants will be enough protection, but if you are going to be somewhere that snakes are very numerous, outdoor outfitters sell inexpensive snake chaps that slide over your pant legs to protect your shins.
- Don't put your hands and feet where you can't see them. Look over a fallen log before you step over it; when climbing a rocky trail, don't reach up onto a sunny boulder overhead. When you're paddling, don't scrape under "strainers" (low trees); there could be a snake in the branches. Use a flashlight when you're walking at night, even on short trips around a campsite.
- If you do see a snake, stay back, outside of striking distance—more than one snake's body length away.
- There's never a good reason to poke a snake with a stick.
- If you see a snake that appears to be dead, do not pick it up. Even a dead snake can bite—through reflex action—and deliver a dose of venom.
- If you're not sure whether a snake is venomous or harmless, play it safe and stay away.
- Teach children to stay away from all snakes.

blood vessels and cause heavy bleeding. When those genes were injected into lab mice, the mice produced antibodies against the venom components. Those antibodies were isolated, purified, and successfully used as a treatment to stop bleeding in other mice that had been injected with viper venom.

Right now, drug manufacturers need large quantities of snake venom to produce antivenin, and that means maintaining large colonies of venomous snakes, which is expensive and dangerous. If the new DNA technique pans out and is economically feasible, drug companies wouldn't have to maintain colonies of live snakes. Instead, scientists could just sequence a synthetic gene in the lab.

Right now, to obtain the large quantities of snake venom needed to make enough antivenin to keep hospitals and research centers safely stocked, snake handlers must milk venomous snakes. The snake handler works with one snake at a time, holding it by the head and positioning it so that its fangs bite through a sterile membrane into a glass beaker. The handler gently strokes the venom glands, and if the snake is in the mood, it will expel its venom into the receptacle. A snake can be milked every few weeks or so.

The drug industry uses snake venom for products other than antivenin. For example, a drug called Ancrod is derived from the venom of Malayan pit vipers. It's an anticoagulant, used to used to treat conditions involving blood clotting, such as deep-vein thrombosis. Ancrod is also being evaluated as a way to improve blood flow after a stroke.

Meanwhile, Integrilin, derived from the venom of the southeastern pygmy rattlesnake, was approved by the FDA in 1998 to treat patients with chest pain, unstable angina, or small heart attacks. Like a daily aspirin, Integrilin has even been shown to reduce a patient's risk of having another heart attack.

Meanwhile, a protein extracted from copperhead venom is showing promise as a potential treatment for breast cancer. The protein, called contortrostatin, significantly reduced tumor growth and metastasis in mice.

3

Habits

A snake's needs are simple. First and foremost, a snake needs food and water—enough to stay alive, and some more in order to grow. Then, since weather can be unpredictable and extreme, it needs ways to keep warm and cool down. Even venomous snakes can have predators, so a snake needs strategies for avoiding danger. And of course, there's an animal's ultimate goal—passing on its genes to the next generation by finding a mate and producing offspring.

In this chapter, we'll take a look at the day-to-day or week-to-week routines of a typical venomous snake: how it moves from place to place, hunts for food, avoids predators, and maintains a comfortable body temperature. We'll also look at the routines that play out over longer time frames, such as shedding skin, finding a mate, seasonal migration, and hibernation.

Movement

For some animals, the days pass in a constant stream of movement. Hummingbirds flit from flower to flower, eating nonstop in order to fuel their metabolic furnaces. Sharks swim steadily across the reef to keep oxygenated water washing over their gills. Snakes, on the other hand, move only when they have to—which isn't very often, since they only need to eat every few weeks.

If you happen to find a snake somewhere out in the wilderness and decide to settle in to spend a few days watching it, chances are you'll be pretty bored. Snakes don't move just for the fun of it . . . they don't play, like otters or wolf cubs do. At zoos, where large numbers of snakes are on display, you'll probably hear the visitors speculating that the colorful serpents behind the glass are really just rubber replicas.

But when a snake does decide to start slithering, it's quite a sight to see. Considering that snakes have no legs or flippers or propulsive appendages of any kind, it can be hard to figure out where their forward momentum comes from.

Physiologists who have studied snake movement closely have determined that the forward momentum comes from the interaction between the snake's vertebrae (the bones that make up its backbone), its hundreds of curved and flexible ribs (which articulate with the vertebrae), its muscles, and the scales on its belly, called belly plates. The free ends of each pair of ribs are connected to a belly plate by a set of muscles. So the ribs, muscles, and belly plate move together in a coordinated way to propel the snake forward.

Biologists have classified snakes' slithering styles into four distinct categories: lateral undulation, or serpentine locomotion; sidewinding; caterpillar, or rectilinear, locomotion; and accordion, or concertina, locomotion.

Lateral undulation is the most common way *all* snakes get around, including all the venomous snakes in the United States. It's a form of movement

Agile without legs, all snakes are good climbers. The cottonmouth, a species that lives near streams, rivers, and wetlands, is a snake you're particularly likely to see basking in the sun on tree limbs that extend out over the water.

that takes advantage of the extreme flexibility of the snake's spine, with its hundreds of vertebrae. But to use this form of movement, generally a snake needs a rough surface, something with little irregularities that its body can push off against.

Lateral undulation works like this: Long muscles run down both sides of the spine. These muscles contract alternately, first on one side of the body, then on the other. The alternate contractions cause the snake's body to bend, first in one direction, then the other, so that it makes a series of smooth, S-shaped curves.

At the same time the body is bending from side to side, the ribs and belly plates push backwards against the rough spots on ground . . . and the snake moves forward. The rough spots are essential; a snake on a smooth surface, such as fresh asphalt or linoleum, will just thrash from side to side, unable to make forward progress. Sea snakes, and land snakes that decide to go for a swim, also use lateral undulation; in this case their bodies push against the resistance of the water.

The rattlesnake called the sidewinder isn't the only snake that moves by sidewinding. This species is just particularly good at it. It also lives in dry, hot, desert sand where sidewinding is an effective way to travel. As a form of loco-motion, sidewinding works especially well on loose surfaces—dry sand or mud as opposed to rock or hard dirt.

A snake that is moving by lateral undulation has its entire body is in con-tact with the ground at all times. A sidewinding snake has only a small part of its body in contact with the ground at any given time, which is useful to pre-vent overheating when traveling over a hot surface. One curious thing about sidewinding is that the actual direction of travel is ninety degrees from the direction in which the snake's body slides. The snake lifts the front of its body up vertically, then heaves it sideways to make progress. A sidewinding snake leaves distinctive J-shaped tracks in the sand.

Caterpillar locomotion is a third and fairly common way that snakes can move. Perhaps you've seen a wooly bear caterpillar crossing a highway, its high, rounded body stretched out in a straight line, carried slowly forward by tiny, almost invisible feet? That's what a snake looks like when it uses this form of locomotion. Heavy-bodied rattlesnakes are particularly likely to chose this mode of travel because it's hard for them to bend side to side. When tim-ber rattlesnakes are on the move in the spring, leaving their winter dens for their lowland summer feeding areas, you often see them crossing mountain roads at a slow, deliberate crawl. Snakes also use caterpillar movement to creep up quietly on prey, or to slide down a narrow rodent burrow.

In lateral undulation, muscles along the sides of the body contract on alter-nate sides. Caterpillar locomotion involves the muscles contracting simultane-ously on both sides of the body, but in a series of short rippling waves that move from one body section backwards to the next.

A fourth kind of movement, rarely used by any of the venomous snakes, is called concertina locomotion. It's a bit like the "chimneying" of a technical

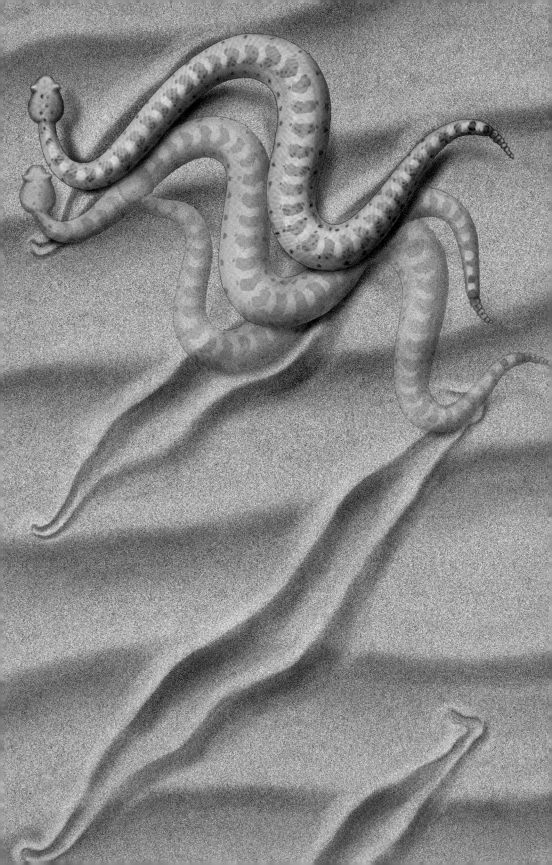

rock climber, useful for moving forward inside tunnels that are too narrow, smooth, or steep for serpentine movement. In concertina locomotion the snake presses a couple of body loops against the walls of the tunnel as an anchor, throws the rest of the body forward, anchors with more loops, and then repeats.

Snakes in motion look as if they are moving at high speeds. But in fact, that's an optical illusion. The flow of the coils past small landmarks on the ground such as pebbles and sticks gives the illusion of speed. Actually, you can run much faster than the fastest snake in the world can crawl. (You can't move faster than a snake can strike, however, so do stay out of striking distance.)

Besides moving along the ground, all snakes can climb boulders, fences, trees, and so on. What's more, all snakes can swim, even desert species. The one thing snakes cannot do is slither backwards.

NASA engineers were so impressed by snakes' locomotor abilities that for a while they had a program where they tried to develop "snakebots" to explore Mars and other worlds. The idea was that robot serpents could go where wheeled robots could not; they could slither into cracks and navigate the roughest terrain. More recently, a team at the University of Michigan designed a snakebot called "Omni Tread," which they are promoting as a tool to conduct hazardous inspections for industry or surveillance for the military.

Feeding

All snakes are carnivores, or meat eaters; there's no such thing as a vegetarian snake. And all snakes swallow their prey whole—no cutting or chewing involved. That's why venom is such a handy adaptation. It's like an injection of meat tenderizer. It jump-starts the digestive process.

Snakes as a group eat a variety of small animals. The menu might include anything from insects and other invertebrates, such as grasshoppers, centipedes, and earthworms; to small rodents such as to mice, rats, squirrels, gophers, prairie dogs, and baby rabbits; to reptiles and amphibians such as frogs, toads, and lizards; to small birds and their eggs. Some snakes eat other snakes, and some species are even cannibalistic. Although many people assume that snakes eat only live prey, some species of venomous snakes are also scavengers and will feed on carrion such as roadkill.

Most venomous snakes are what ecologists call generalists, as opposed to specialists. They're not picky. They're willing to scarf down a variety of prey.

Facing page: Sidewinding is a mode of locomotion that works well on soft desert sand. The snake grips the sand with just the rear edge of its body while throwing forward the leading coil. This coil makes contact with the sand, and then, as the rest of the body catches up, the forward-thrusting motion repeats. Sidewinding leaves behind distinctive parallel "J-shaped" tracks. Sidewinding keeps snakes cool in the desert heat because only a tiny portion of the body touches the sand at any one time.

They don't just go after, say, meadow voles and nothing but meadow voles. Typically, young snakes take small prey items, such as insects and small rodents, because that's what they're capable of swallowing. As a snake grows larger, it can handle prey with a larger diameter.

Experts who have considered the competition report that the front-fanged venomous snakes are probably the most efficient predators on earth. For other predators, taking down even the smallest, meekest prey animal can sometimes be risky. Owls get scratched and bitten by their rodent prey. Wolves get gored by moose. Even lions get kicked by zebra. But because they are equipped with deadly venom, snakes simply strike, release their prey, wait for it to die, and then slide on over for a meal. It's the ultimate low-risk way to hunt.

Snakes use a variety of senses to land a meal, including sight, smell, touch, and (in the case of pit vipers) infrared heat detection. They put these senses to work in two general hunting strategies: ambush hunting and active pursuit.

Ready to strike . . . Moments earlier, this timber rattlesnake was resting in a loose coil, motionless but alert. Now, having drawn a bead on its prey, its head is up in the attack position, like a gun that's cocked and ready to fire.

The strike! The snake thrusts its body forward, stabs its fangs deep into the body of its prey, injects its venom, and then releases the unlucky animal—all in a fraction of a second.

In ambush hunting, a snake takes advantage of the fact that small rodents and lizards are creatures of habit and spend their whole lives within a patch of turf called a home range. Within this range, these animals tend to travel along well-defined paths they have created for themselves. Often a travel route will lead along the top of a fallen log, or up a tree trunk, or through a tunnel in tall grass, or through a crevice between tall boulders.

The snake may use its sense of smell, taste, or sight to locate one of these travel routes. Then it sets up the ambush. It settles in a shady spot where its mottled scale pattern blends with the vegetation or soil. Then, it waits . . . for hours or sometimes days without moving, until a mouse or lizard approaches.

Timber rattlesnakes in particular are know for setting up ambushes along the fallen logs that mice use as runways, or at the base of trees where squirrels or chipmunks are likely to descend. The snake will rest, neatly coiled, with its head up, perpendicular to the predicted path of travel, perfectly still, ready to make the intercept.

The snake may detect its prey using any of its senses. It may see the movement of its prey, feel the vibration of its feet striking the ground or the log, use its heat-sensing pits to feel the heat of the animal's body, or—by flicking its tongue and tasting the air—sense its approach as a chemical signal. When the

MYTH OR FACT?

Snakes strike only from a coiled position.

Myth. Snakes can strike from any position. Just because a rattlesnake is not coiled up does not mean it will not strike you. Stay safe–stay away!

Bite and release is the rattlesnake's strategy with warm-blooded prey. A strike to the thoracic region injects poison into an area of the body well-supplied with blood vessels. This chipmunk will run away, but the venom will spread quickly throughout its body—causing blood cells and body tissues to break down. It will collapse and die within minutes, usually after traveling less than a hundred feet. Meanwhile, the snake will have been tracking down its meal by tasting the air for its scent trail.

prey is in range, the snake strikes. Most often it drives the venom into the region of the thorax, which has the most blood vessels.

At this point, if the prey item is a warm-blooded creature such as a mouse, the snake is still somewhat at risk. Rodents have sharp teeth and could fight back. So, the snake simply releases its prey, which then runs off, trying to escape. But there's not much point in running. It's received a deadly dose of venom, and the snake is already tracking it, flicking its tongue rapidly in a process called strike-induced chemosensory searching. Usually, a mouse dies within ten minutes, having traveled less than a hundred feet. Swinging its head side to side and flicking its tongue to catch the odor trail, the snake tracks down its meal.

Snakes don't always strike and release. If their prey is a fellow ectotherm—a lizard, snake, frog, toad, or insect—they're more likely to strike and hang on. Ectotherms are harder to track by scent if released, and venom doesn't take effect on them as quickly as it would on a warm-blooded animal, so they are more likely to run a long way off. Researchers studying pygmy rattlesnakes in central Florida tell of coming across one of these small snakes poised at the base of a tree. They looked up, and several feet above the snake dangled a dead *Anolis* lizard, clinging to the tree by one claw. They concluded that the snake had struck and released the lizard, and the lizard had then climbed up out of the snake's reach and died.

Snakes will also strike and hang on if the prey is a bird or a bat. After all, if released, these creatures will fly, leaving no scent trail at all.

Rattlesnakes that are very hungry abandon the ambush-hunting strategy and instead use active foraging. Coral snakes use this strategy routinely. They act somewhat like hunting dogs as they root around in the leaf litter and forest debris, poking their heads into cavities and under decaying leaves and slithering down into rodent burrows, all while looking for the small lizards and snakes that are their main prey. After striking, coral snakes hang onto their prey until their neurotoxic venom induces paralysis.

In many rattlesnake species, and also copperheads and cottonmouths, the very young snakes use a hunting strategy that's halfway between ambush and active foraging. They do lie in wait for their prey, but they actively lure that prey to their hiding place, using a kind of bait—specifically, the tips of their tails. In all of these species, young snakes are born with brightly colored tail tips—either yellow or green. The tail tip stands out like a beacon in dim forest light. The young snakes simply lie still and wiggle their tail tips like fishing lures to attract frogs or toads within striking range.

Snakes don't need to go hunting very often. Since they are ecothermic and don't rely on their own metabolism to generate heat, they don't need to eat every day, the way most mammals and birds do. They can go for days, weeks, or, in some cases, months, depending on the circumstances. Adult rattlesnakes in warm desert habitats may be perfectly satisfied with about half a dozen rodents per year.

Shedding Skin

You may not realize it, but you shed bits of your skin constantly, a few cells here, a few cells there. You probably don't notice it, except perhaps in the winter, when your skin gets dry and flaky. A snake, on the other hand, never sheds just a few cells. Instead, a few times a year, a snake shed its entire outermost layer of skin—the whole thing, all at once, starting at the nose and going down to the tail. It's a bit like rolling a tube sock off from the knee down to the toes.

Why do snakes shed the entire covering all at once? A snake's scales are rich in keratin, a tough, horny material that does a great job protecting the body from rocks and thorns and bites and scratches. On the other hand, keratin is not very elastic. To grow bigger, the snake literally has to get rid of its old body covering and grow in a new one that's a better fit.

Shedding is sometimes called molting or sloughing. The scientific term for the process is *ecdysis,* from the Greek meaning "to strip off." Snakes may shed their skin from one to six times a year. The exact frequency depends on a number of factors: how old the snake is (young snakes grow faster than old snakes, so they shed more frequently), how well-fed it is (it takes calories to make new skin, so well-fed snakes shed more frequently than poorly nourished snakes), and the local climate (it takes energy to shed, so snakes in warm climates shed more frequently than snakes in cold regions). Rattlesnakes in North America's

Snakes shed their skin to grow larger, and to refresh a worn-out layer of skin. The old skin comes off as one continuous piece, starting at the nose and rolling back along the body like a tube sock.

desert regions typically shed about three times a year. Timber rattlesnakes in cool regions are more likely to shed just once a year.

How often a snake sheds also depends on how active that snake has been. A snake that has been traveling a lot and eating a lot during a warm spell is more likely to shed than a snake that has lying low during cool weather. Injured snakes, or snakes with parasites or a skin infection, may shed again and again, as their bodies try to repair skin damage.

Snakes that hibernate during the winter tend to shed right after they emerge in spring. Snakes often shed just before they mate, and female rattlesnakes, which bear live young, often shed just before giving birth.

When a snake is getting ready to shed, its skin starts to look dull, and its eyes appear cloudy, almost a milky blue. This change is caused by fluid buildup between the old, outside layer of skin and the new layer forming beneath it. With its eyes clouded, the snake can't see very well, so it doesn't hunt. Instead, it finds a place to hole up and wait. Snakes are likely to be pretty irritable before shedding as well.

Somehow, the snake knows when it's time . . . when the new layer of skin is complete and the old layer has separated. It starts rubbing its nose against a rock or some other rough surface to loosen the old layer. The skin pulls back around the lips and snout, and as the snake crawls forward, its old skin peels back, inside out, all in one piece. This process may look uncomfortable, but it doesn't hurt the snake at all—it's comparable to getting your nails clipped. Who knows if it's part of a whole cleanse and refresh ritual, but snakes often defecate right after they shed, and they also tend to drink lots of water to rehydrate right after shedding.

Although coral snakes and rattlesnakes have beautiful scale patterns, a cast skin is colorless. That's because snake skin is made up of two layers: the outer epidermis and the inner dermis. The pigment cells that give snakes their distinctive colors are in the inner dermis layer, which is not shed. Only the epidermis, the layer that contains horny keratin that forms the scales, comes off. So even though the shed skin retains the shape of the snake, it is completely transparent.

Rattling

Rattlesnakes are unique among all snakes for the rattles at the tips of their tails. Scientists think rattles evolved as a way for snakes to tell potential predators "back off!" Contrary to folklore, there's no evidence that rattlesnakes use their rattles to attract mates or warn other snakes of danger (and mother snakes do not use their rattles to lull their babies to sleep).

Each time a rattlesnake sheds, it adds one rattle segment to its tail. The process works like this: Baby snakes are born with no rattle at all; instead, they have a structure at the tip of the tail called a prebutton. A few days after birth, the little snake sheds for the first time and molts the prebutton, revealing a structure underneath called the button, which is now at the surface.

Rattlesnakes are unique—they're the only snakes in the world that have rattles. This cross-section of a rattle from a western diamondback rattlesnake shows the internal structure. Each time the snake sheds its skin, a new segment is added at the base of the rattle; it interlocks with the previous segment. Rattles probable evolved as a way to warn hooved animals "Don't step on me!" Some island populations of rattlesnakes have no rattles.

MYTH OR FACT?
A rattlesnake adds one rattle per year.

Myth. A rattlesnake adds one rattle each time it sheds its skin. A snake may shed anywhere from once a year to three times a year or more, depending on the weather and how much the snake is eating. A snake is always adding rattles, but it is always losing them too. A rattle might get knocked off in combat with another snake or get worn off as the snake brushes past a rock.

So the number of rattles is not a reliable indicator of age, although a snake with a lot of rattles is probably a pretty old snake.

At the second shed, the first rattle segment pushes up beneath the button. With a button plus one rattle segment, the snake can now rattle. Each time the snake sheds, a new rattle segment pushes up to join the other segments. They're a bit like a stack of interlocked straw hats.

As the rattle gets longer, it also gets louder. A big rattlesnake's rattle can peak at a frequency of 5,000 to 8,000 Hz, which is equivalent to the siren of an ambulance, and can be as loud as 60 to 80 decibels from a distance of one meter. This is comparable to the noise of city traffic.

Not all rattlesnakes are loud, though. The tiny pygmy rattlesnake earns the nickname "buzzworm" for its soft rattle, a faint whirring sound often mistaken for an insect's raspy call.

A rattlesnake on the move holds the tip of its tail vertical to protect its rattle. Even so, over time, as the snake slides over rocks, past boulders, and through bushes, rattle segments at the very tip of the structure are likely to break off. So, even though rattlesnakes can live for fifteen years or more and may molt three or more times a year, it's quite rare to see a snake in the wild with more than ten rattle segments.

Avoiding Predators

You might think venomous snakes wouldn't have to worry about predators. But even snakes with a deadly bite are vulnerable when they are young and small. Many kinds of carnivores will attack a snake. House cats and feral cats attack snakes that live around human habitation. Some kinds of hawks and various species of owls will dive on a snake if they spy one out in the open. In desert environments, coyotes, peccaries, roadrunners, and ravens all make meals of rattlesnakes. Cottonmouths and massasaugas, which live in wetland habitat, have to look out for otter, mink, and large wading birds. Other predators include raccoons, skunks, bobcats, shrikes, and whipsnakes.

A snake's first reaction to danger is to freeze, hoping to avoid being noticed; it will only strike as a last resort. A few predators, including kingsnakes, indigo snakes, and opossums, are actually immune to rattlesnake venom and don't have to worry about getting bitten.

Besides their patterned scales for camouflage, venomous snakes do have a few other tricks to fall back on. When their dusky camouflage doesn't fool an attacker, cottonmouths usually retreat to safety. Typically, they'll try to escape down a handy burrow, under a streambank, or into the water.

If there's no clear avenue of escape, a cottonmouth will try to run off the attacker with a scary defensive display. It coils up, vibrates its tail, and gapes its mouth wide open to reveal the startling white lining. If the predator persists, not only will the cottonmouth strike, but it will also squirt smelly musk from glands at either side of the base of the tail. Timber rattlesnakes and pygmy rattlesnakes also use musk as a defense.

Eastern coral snakes have the opposite of camouflage. Their bright red, yellow, and black scales are a widely recognized signal throughout the natural world: "Watch out! Poison!" The trouble is, there are always inexperienced predators who haven't yet learned what this color pattern means.

So eastern coral snakes, like cottonmouths, tend to respond to a perceived threat by trying to run away and hide—diving into an underground burrow or wriggling under a pile of dead leaves. If there's no good hiding place at hand, the coral snake, like the cottonmouth, has a strategy to scare off attackers. It flattens its body along the ground, with its head hidden underneath its coils, and then raises its tail as if the tail were the head. When the predator attacks the tail, the snake whips out its real head and lunges for a bite.

The closely related Arizona coral snake takes this subterfuge one step farther. If disturbed by a possible predator, this species also raises the tip of its tail, waving it around like a fake head. But at the same time, this snake turns the lining of its cloaca inside out to make a sharp popping sound. Scientists aren't sure why—or even exactly how—the snake does this, but it does seem likely to startle an attacker.

Keeping Warm or Cool

Mammals and birds are endothermic and make their own body heat. Through metabolic processes, they maintain a constant body temperature. Snakes, on the other hand, are ectothermic. They have to rely, ultimately, on the sun as a source of warmth.

There's a tendency to assume that mammals are at the evolutionary pinnacle and so being an endotherm must be somehow better than being an ectotherm. But if you think about it from an animal's perspective, there are some advantages to being an ectotherm. Since you don't need to burn calories just to keep you warm, you only need about a tenth as much food as a mammal of about the same size. Since you don't need much food, you don't have to eat all that often, and that means you don't have to catch all that much food. You can go for a long time between meals. So you can have a pretty laid-back life.

Many people assume that being ectothermic means the animal takes on the temperature of the environment it finds itself in. That's not exactly true. Ectotherms do rely on the environment as a source of heat, but they also regulate their body temperature through their behavior within that environment. Through its behavior a snake can manage to stay significantly warmer (or significantly cooler) than the outside air—for example, by seeking out a protected sunny spot, or a cool burrow. It's a good thing, too. Otherwise they'd have a tough time living in the scorching desert or in places with freezing winter weather—places where they do live quite successfully.

In general, most snakes must maintain their body temperature between 53 and 90 degrees Fahrenheit. Anything much hotter or colder than that could have an impact on the snake's ability to move, catch prey, escape from predators, digest its food, and grow bigger. Optimal body temperature is around 86 degrees F. A body temperature much colder than 41 or much hotter than 108 degrees F is usually fatal to a snake.

A timber rattler basks in the sun. Snakes cannot generate their own body heat through metabolic processes, so they bask to warm up—to prepare their muscles for movement, as an aid to digestion, or, in spring, when males are developing sperm or females are incubating young.

The cottonmouth shares its habitat with the harmless and somewhat similar-looking water snake. You can tell them apart by the way they swim. Notice how this cottonmouth floats high in the water—as it swims, the length of its body is visible above the surface. Water snakes are less buoyant and tend to swim with only their heads above the surface.

Every snake's skin is well supplied with nerve endings that sense the temperature. The snake constantly monitors the temperature around it and moves to a different location depending on its thermoregulatory needs.

Insects such as dragonflies also bask in the sun to warm up and prepare their muscles for flight. But when a snake basks, it is not necessarily getting ready to move. Basking may just be a way to boost the body's internal processes. In temperate zones in spring, for example, when male timber rattlesnakes emerge from their dens, they bask for hours, but not because they're getting ready to crawl off to feed. Basking helps them develop a new layer of skin; it also helps new sperm to mature.

When a snake first emerges from a burrow and wants to warm up fast, it may lie in the sun with its body all stretched out. For maximum exposure to the sun, the snake may even flatten its body by spreading the free ends of the ribs so more surface area is exposed. But flattening out makes a snake pretty conspicuous, so once it gets a little bit warm, it will usually coil up. To get maximum sun exposure in a coiled position, it will make the coils neat and concentric, not overlapping. Snakes often return to the same basking site over and over again.

A snake that needs to cool off will often retreat into an underground burrow or the shelter of a crevice in a rock. The cottonmouth, a water-loving snake, will dive into a stream or swamp and sink under a log or streambank with its body mostly submerged.

Snakes switch not only their position, but the timing of their activity pattern to regulate their temperature. If summer days are very hot, for example, snakes will switch from daytime to nighttime hunting, if that helps them to stay cool. (This is in contrast to mammals and birds, which are always either nocturnal or day-active, no matter what the weather.)

Hibernation

Snakes can't maintain their body temperature in extremely cold weather, so populations that live where temperatures fall below freezing for long periods of time pass this cold period in a state of inactivity referred to as hibernation.

Most of the North American rattlesnake species spend at least some time hibernating. Northern populations hibernate longer than southern populations. The eastern coral snake hibernates underground everywhere in its range except Florida. Arizona coral snakes hibernate from about October to March.

Hibernation for snakes is a bit different than hibernation for mammals such as woodchucks and bears. Hibernating mammals spend the summer eating extra food in order to build up a layer of fat. The fat sustains them while they hibernate; true hibernation for mammals involves slowing the body's metabolic cycle and lowering the body temperature.

Snakes don't necessarily need to build up fat reserves in order to hibernate, although some snakes do fatten up before winter. And since they don't regulate their body temperature metabolically the rest of the year, this isn't a factor in hibernation.

Snakes hibernate in dens—protected locations, such as an underground mammal's burrow (occupied or unoccupied), hollow tree stump, or crevice in a rock pile. Different snake species have different preferences for den sites, but all will accept a variety of locations. Usually a den is situated in a sunny location, often on a mountain slope that faces either south or west.

Research shows that snakes return to the exact same den site each fall, year after year. No one knows exactly how they do it; the current hypothesis is that snakes follow scent trails laid down by other snakes when they left the den the previous spring (this would explain how snakes born that summer find their way to a den site they have never seen—they follow the scent of their own species). Another possibility is that snakes navigate by the sun or by landmarks.

Timber rattlesnakes emerge from their rocky dens in spring. Preferred den sites are on sunny, south-facing slopes; good dens are in short supply and in some locations as many as one hundred to two hundred rattlesnakes may share the same den site.

Good den sites are in short supply, so often lots of snakes will use the same site. Timber rattlesnakes may gather in groups of more than a hundred, and western rattlesnakes can squeeze as many as thousand snakes into a sizeable den.

It's not always snakes of the same species occupying a single den either. In the East, for example, timber rattlesnakes, copperheads, and rat snakes often share a den. In the West, whipsnakes and gopher snakes bunk in with western rattlesnakes. Snakes will lie all huddled together in a pile. They can't share body heat, but the skin-to-skin contact may help prevent moisture loss.

Depending on the weather, some snakes spend more time hibernating than they do being active. Timber rattlers in upstate New York hibernate for more than seven months of the year. Eastern diamondbacks in northern Florida, on the other hand, hibernate only in December and January. Pygmy rattlesnakes in central Florida never hibernate; they are active all year round.

During hibernation, snakes are in a state that biologist call torpor. They're lethargic, but they can move a little. They don't store up food and eat it during the winter, they don't go out to feed, and they don't mate. But if there's a winter warm spell, they will rouse from their torpor and leave the den to bask in the sun for a bit.

Hibernation is how snakes in cold places make it through the winter months. But snakes may also become inactive in summer in places where temperatures get very high. Torpor during very hot summer weather is called aestivation. Desert-dwelling rattlesnakes aestivate in underground burrows during the hottest weeks of summer. Cottonmouths in the Southwest also aestivate in high summer when it's very hot and dry and there's hardly any prey around.

Migration

Some species of venomous snake live in different habitats at different times of the year, and move back and forth between them. Timber rattlesnakes, for example, hang out in their rocky hilltop dens in winter, but travel to lowland meadows to forage in the summer. These seasonal movements between one habitat and the other are called migration.

Other animals that migrate—birds, fish, caribou—tend to travel very long distances, from hundreds to thousands of miles. In contrast, the migrations that snakes undertake are fairly short. Migrating snakes typically travel anywhere from a few hundred yards to a couple of miles.

Reproduction

Anchovies swim in vast schools. Crows roost for the night in flapping, squawking flocks. Bison graze in thundering herds. Snakes, on the other hand, like to go solo. Each snake lives most of its life alone—hunting for itself, defending itself, sleeping alone.

So when it's time to find a mate, how do a male snake and a female snake ever find each other? In many species, the female releases chemical signals called pheromones from her skin and scent glands in her tail. The scent lets any males within smelling distance know that she is receptive to mating.

Among rattlesnakes, mating happens at a fairly advanced age. Many rattlesnake species are not sexually mature until they are three or four years old, and some are considerably older before they can mate for the first time. Among timber rattlesnakes, for example, males don't mate until they are four to six years old, and females wait until they are seven to ten years old.

Coral snakes don't wait so long; they are ready to reproduce at one to two years of age.

Snakes that live in temperate zones usually mate soon after they emerge from hibernation. That means most snakes mate in the spring, although some may mate in the fall, in which case the female may store the sperm and not allow her eggs to be fertilized until spring. During the breeding season, male rattlesnakes will wander around, actively looking—or rather sniffing—for females. If one male snake comes across another male who has already claimed a female, the two males will fight over her in a highly ritualized form of combat. Some observers report that this combat looks like a dance, or maybe arm wrestling. The two males rear up on their tails, then twine the front parts of their bodies around one another and engage in a violent shoving match, each one trying to push the other's head and trunk onto the ground. The loser slithers away, and the winner gets to mate with the female. Biting and injuries are rare.

It's also pretty rare for human observers to come across snakes mating in the wild, so the courtship rituals of most species have not been well described.

Courtship is probably different for each species but with some shared elements. The male needs to be on top of or next to the female, and his cloaca has to come in contact with hers as he inserts his hemipenis. As in mammals and birds, the male may bite the female on the neck or head, and she may indicate that she is ready to mate by lifting her tail. Snakes are not monogamous. Either partner may go on to take other partners later in the mating season.

Coral snakes are egg-laying snakes. The female lays her tiny, leathery-shelled eggs in sand or leaf litter, covers them up, and leaves them to incubate on their own. She doesn't guard them or care for them in any way. Rattlesnakes do not lay eggs; they bear their young alive. Inside female rattlesnakes, a structure that resembles a primitive placenta develops. It helps to nourish the tiny snakes.

Young colubrid and elapid snakes are usually more brightly colored than their parents. Newly hatched or newborn, young venomous snakes can see, crawl, and feed on their own, and their bite is already venomous. They don't rely on their parents, and their parents don't provide any tender loving care for them, as far as scientists can tell.

Among most vipers, it's typical for the female to bear young only every other year. That's because, while she is carrying the developing young snakes

Most snakes lay eggs, but female rattlesnakes give birth to live young—after a three-month pregnancy. As the embryos develop inside their mother, they get nutrients from the yolk mass and a primitive placenta. After birth, the young snakes may stay with the female for a week or so; whether she actually defends them is a subject of scientific debate.

inside her body, she eats fairly little. The next year, she takes a year off from reproduction and eats a lot to build her body back up. Given that females breed only every other year, that means in any given year, only half of the females are available to the males. It's no wonder the males fight over mates.

Good Mothers?

One hotly debated question in the world of rattlesnake research right now is whether females care for their young after birth. For all of the U.S. rattlesnakes—notably pygmy and black-tailed rattlesnakes—there have been some sightings of females staying near the young for about a week after birth, until the baby snakes' first molt. Are these females defending their young from danger? So far, the evidence is inconclusive.

In the 1980s, one researcher tried a simple experiment. He walked toward female rattlesnakes and noted how they reacted. What he noticed was that pregnant females let him get very close before starting to rattle—or they'd slide away into a burrow. But females with newborn young behaved differently. They got very agitated and started rattling while he was still some distance away. He interpreted this behavior as maternal care—defending the young.

More recently, a research team in Florida tried the same thing with mother snakes and a natural predator. They let caged pygmy rattlesnakes see a snake called a southern black racer, which eats the little rattlesnakes, and watched and noted the rattlesnakes' reactions. Pygmy rattlesnakes that had recently born young had very strong reactions. Eighty-three percent of them rattled or puffed up their bodies. When a similar number of females that had no baby snakes were tested, only a third of them reacted to the racers.

These researchers also devised a lab experiment to test whether mother and young had feelings for one another. They put sixteen pygmy rattlesnake families in individual glass aquaria: mother on one side, young on the other, separated by a barrier. The only connection between the two sides was a tunnel lined with rows of nails so that only the baby snakes could fit between the spaces.

Then, the researchers waited to see what happened. At the end of three days, most of the little snakes had crawled through the tunnel to be with their mothers—not the result you'd expect if there were no particular attraction to mom.

The experiment worked in the other direction, too. When the barrier was a partition so high that only the mother snake was big enough to crawl over it, twelve out of sixteen moms crossed over to their young.

4

Conservation Issues

The very first flag of the fledgling United States was not the familiar Stars and Stripes. It was a mustard-yellow banner showing a coiled timber rattlesnake, mouth open, ready to strike. Above the snake was the slogan, "Don't Tread on Me." It was a potent symbol of colonial America's resistance to the British.

At the very moment when Americans were embracing rattlesnakes as a political symbol, however, they were also putting a bounty on rattlesnakes' heads and hunting them down like vermin. Indeed, each spring, no less a renowned personage than the Boston minister Cotton Mather would give a sermon in which he told his flock it was their Christian duty to hunt down and kill venomous serpents.

This attitude—that venomous snakes are something to be wiped from the earth—persisted well into the twentieth century. Every state that was home to venomous snakes offered cash payments for dead snakes. People believed that human intervention was absolutely essential to keep snake populations low. Otherwise, it was thought, snakes would multiply rapidly and swarm over the country like a plague of locusts.

Hunting down venomous snakes could be lucrative. Wisconsin paid a bounty of one dollar per rattle on a rattlesnake's tail (up to five dollars per snake). With this motivation, one bounty hunter was reported to have killed fifty-seven hundred timber rattlesnakes in a single season. In 1975, the year the state stopped paying bounties, the massasauga was placed on the state endangered species list.

New York paid not by the rattle but by the snake—and the compensation of five dollars per carcass even extended to embryos cut from the bellies of pregnant females. Bounties were paid in New York until 1971. Hunters would look for dens where snakes congregated in the winter and clear out hundreds at a time.

In general, people saw killing venomous snakes as a positive thing to do. Ranchers thought that their livestock would be safer with fewer snakes on grazing land. And parents certainly didn't want snakes on their property, threatening their children and pets. This attitude continues today. The timber rattlesnake is listed as a threatened species in New York State. Yet an acquaintance who is well educated and considers herself sensitive to environmental issues once told me that when she saw a timber rattlesnake in her driveway, she deliberately drove her car over it.

In the 1970s, with the growth of the ecology movement, scientists came to appreciate the valuable role that venomous snakes play in ecosystems as top predators. For example, they can help to control populations of rats or mice, which can damage crops and carry disease.

Researchers have also come to understand that snakes don't need humans to regulate their populations. Natural factors such as predators, weather, and disease do the job just fine. But over the years in North American, uncounted numbers of venomous snakes have been killed by bounty hunters. More recently, snakes have been taken from the wild for the pet trade, or collected during so-called rattlesnake roundups, then sold as a source of meat, leather, souvenirs, or antivenin.

Many more have died on the road, run over by cars. And more have probably died, or populations have simply dwindled, because snake habitat has been developed. Wetland feeding areas have been ditched and dredged, winter den sites have been broken apart by snake hunters, summer feeding sites have turned into housing developments or shopping malls. All these changes have brought some populations of venomous snakes to dangerously low levels.

A SNAKE-FREE YARD

So you live in rattlesnake habitat, but you want to work in your garden, and you want to let your kids play outside. You don't have to kill the snakes! Just discourage them from moving into your yard.

Rattlesnakes will go where there is food. Their preferred prey is small rodents. Keep small rodents away from your house, and you are less likely to attract rattlesnakes.

- Make sure your garbage cans are tightly covered.
- Feed birds only in cold weather, when snakes are dormant. The seeds that drop from bird feeders will also attract small rodents. Clean up the bird feeder site before warm weather arrives.
- Get rid of "rodent hotels" such as woodpiles, rock piles, or brush piles that offer shelter to mice and rats.

Loss of Habitat

American's population was about seventy-six million in 1900. Today, the head count stands at more than three hundred million. More people means more cities and roads, more land used for farmland, more forests logged over, more swampy spots drained, more open spaces developed . . . in sum, less wild land. Population growth necessarily has an impact on wildlife, including venomous snakes.

In the South, cottonmouths and massasauga rattlesnakes, which rely on habitat associated with wetlands, are two species adversely affected by the draining of swamps and marshes for development. In the Southeast, only fragments of the pine-woods habitat of the eastern diamondback remain—the rest has been logged over, planted as tree farms, converted to croplands, or developed. In the Northeast, the forest-dwelling timber rattlesnake and copperhead have been affected by forest fragmentation, as once-continuous woodlots have been carved up for housing lots and shopping centers. Western grasslands have been plowed up for crops or overgrazed by cattle, ruining habitat for the prairie rattlesnake.

In some cases, what might seem like improvement to a plot of land can actually be bad for snakes. In the arid Southwest, for example, expanses of desert land have been converted to cropland through irrigation. But that means habitat for desert-dwelling rattlesnake species has been destroyed.

Sometimes the issue is not just loss of habitat, but loss of a very particular aspect of the habitat. During the winter, eastern diamondbacks in Georgia and Alabama retreat into the capacious underground burrows dug by gopher tortoises. These burrows, which can be six feet deep and fifteen feet long, may shelter a number of rattlesnakes simultaneously (and not just rattlesnakes—scientists have tallied more than three hundred different animal species that rely on either occupied or abandoned gopher tortoise burrows for shelter).

The trouble is that snake hunters often go after the denning snakes by pouring gasoline into a burrow. This makes the snakes come out, but it also permanently ruins the burrow as a home for the tortoise, other snakes, and any other animals. It takes the tortoise years to dig a new burrow of comparable size. In the meantime, snakes in the area are left without a winter shelter.

Cars

Roads make up an estimated one percent of the land area in the continental United States. That sounds like a small proportion, but the impact on snakes can be large if a road happens to run through their home range. Getting run over by cars, whether deliberately or accidentally, is a major source of mortality for venomous snakes.

Snakes end up on road surfaces for two reasons. First, it may be that the snake simply must cross the road because it transects the route the snake needs to take between its winter den site, usually high on a rocky mountain-

A cottonmouth uses caterpillar locomotion (straight-line, rather than undulating, movement) to cross a road. Encounters with cars are a major cause of mortality for snakes; studies show that drivers will avoid other reptiles but aim straight for snakes on the road.

side, and its summer feeding grounds, often in a grassy lowland meadow. Snakes also crawl onto roads for another reason: it's a good place for a snake to get warm during cooler weather.

A snake's mottled scale pattern may give it perfect camouflage in its natural habitat, but against black asphalt it stands out—and, unfortunately, all too many drivers take aim. This has been documented by scientific research. A few years ago, students at Southeastern Louisiana University conducted a study of how traffic affects reptiles. One question they wanted to answer was whether drivers targeted snakes in particular. They placed either a rubber snake or a rubber turtle in the middle of a busy road, then hid behind bushes to watch what happened. The student researchers found that drivers were likely to swerve to avoid the turtles, but tended to aim straight for the snakes and drive over them.

In another study, conducted in Idaho, researchers checked to see whether or not real live snakes actually had success crossing a road. They cruised along ten-kilometer segments of a state highway, back and forth, night after night, one summer in 2004, watching for snakes on the road. Their conclusion? "Traffic volume of less than ten vehicles per hour was sufficient to cause a hundred percent mortality on some nights."

Rattlesnake Roundups

It's not clear who came up with the idea, but the first-ever rattlesnake roundup was held nearly seventy years ago in Okeene, Oklahoma. The event is still a popular yearly tradition in this small town of about twelve hundred. The town of Sweetwater, Texas, which launched its roundup in 1958, today bills the event as the "world's largest," attracting about thirty-five thousand visitors a year to a town with a population of just eleven thousand.

Many other communities—mostly in southern and southwestern states, including Georgia, Alabama, Florida, Arkansas, Mississippi, Texas, and New Mexico—also hold roundups. Usually, nonprofit civic associations such as the Jaycees or Kiwanis clubs organize the events, giving them the appearance of social do-gooding.

Rattlesnake roundups were in fact originally promoted as a community service. The idea was to protect people and cattle by having hunters go out to round up and remove from the land as many rattlesnakes as possible. Some of the organizations that sponsor roundups also say that venom is extracted from the snakes and eventually goes for scientific research or to make antivenin.

Rattlesnake roundups resemble firemen's carnivals or small county fairs. They may include parades, beauty queens, food vendors, and carnival rides. But snakes are the main attraction. In the weeks or months leading up to the event, which often lasts several days, people go into local wild areas—woods, fields, or deserts—and catch as many rattlesnakes as they can. Then, during the roundup itself, there are prizes and trophies for the longest and heaviest snake, for the most snakes caught by one person, and so on.

Meanwhile, rattlesnake chili, barbecue, burgers, and the like may be for sale, along with rattlesnake-themed souvenirs. And visitors can interact with the snakes in a variety of ways. Some roundups have "sacking contests," where a pile of rattlesnakes is released into the bed of a pickup or some other enclosed area, and contestants compete against the clock to pin and grab the snakes and stuff them into bags. At a few roundups, you can pay for the thrill of chopping off a snake's head. And a few roundups still feature daredevil shows, where the handler may, for example, harass a snake till it coils up, then set the coiled snake on his head. Or he may slide into a sleeping bag full of rattlesnakes, then let someone shake the bag. Often billed as "safety talks," daredevil shows actually showcase unsafe practices that sometimes end up with the handler being bitten.

At the end of a roundup, the snakes are sold, mostly to commercial processors in Texas, Oklahoma, and Florida. Rattlesnake skins are tanned into leather which is then fashioned into hatbands, wallets, western boots, and similar items. Snake heads, fangs, and rattles also are made into trinkets.

Wildlife biologists object to rattlesnake roundups on several points. First, they refute the argument made by event organizers that roundups are useful for controlling local snake populations. Evidence shows that collectors often bring snakes to a roundup from quite far away—even out of state. For example, western diamondback rattlesnakes have shown up at some Kansas roundups, even though the species is not native to Kansas.

Biologists also say that there's no scientific evidence to support the idea that we need roundups to control snake numbers. In the United States, hunting is helpful to control the population of certain species such as deer because deer reproduce quickly, and because their natural predators have been mostly wiped out. Rattlesnakes, on the other hand, reproduce very slowly. Most take years to reach sexual maturity, and when they do reach reproductive age, females have just a few young in each litter. Venomous snakes don't need humans to control their populations because they face plenty of predators when they are young—hawks, owls, coyotes, skunks, other snakes—not to mention man-made dangers such as cars, guns, shovels, pollution, and habitat loss. Rattlesnake roundups put extra pressure on snake populations that are already challenged to stay at replacement level.

As for the argument made by roundup organizers that snakes in the wild are a threat to livestock and human life, government statistics show that deaths due to snakebite are quite rare among cattle and horses. The number of people bitten accidentally is also quite small. Rattlesnake roundups may actually increase the number of humans bitten when people who attend these events indulge in "quick-bagging" and "free-handling."

Animal welfare advocates also object to rattlesnake roundups because the snakes may be treated in a variety of inhumane ways, starting with the hunting techniques. Some hunters use a pole tipped with fish hooks to pull snakes from their dens. These hooks can cause terrible skin and internal injuries. Other hunters may force snakes out of their dens by pouring in gasoline, liquid fertilizer, or other volatile chemicals. Not only does this destroy the den for future generations of snakes, but some snakes don't make it out and are killed outright. Other animals that may share the dens, including a variety of other snakes, frogs, toads, moles, shrews, and prairie dogs—the list goes on and on—can also be killed or poisoned or lose their homes. Gassing is now illegal in Georgia and Florida, but it is difficult to police in the backwoods.

As the snakes leave their dens, snake hunters grab them near the back of the head with metal poles called snake tongs. An expert snake handler knows to then support the snake's body, but hunters often do not, and as a snake thrashes around, the weight of its own body can injure its spinal cord. Hunters often collect snakes months in advance of roundups, and they may keep them in unprotected, overcrowded outdoor pens, with no food and little water.

Roundup organizers sometimes assert that their events provide a service by collecting rattlesnake venom, which can be used to make the antidote for snakebites. If you go to a roundup, you may, in fact, see snakes being milked for their venom. However, the U.S. Food and Drug Administration has strict guidelines for the conditions under which venom must be collected in order to be used to make antivenin. For example, the container must be sterile and covered by a sterile membrane, since venom degrades rapidly when exposed to air. These conditions generally aren't met in the typical rattlesnake roundup venom-milking exhibit. It's unlikely that a U.S. producer of antivenin would want to purchase venom collected at a roundup.

Catch-and-Release Roundups

As many as ten communities in Pennsylvania hold rattlesnake roundups each year. Some of these roundups have been a local tradition for as long as fifty years. But roundups in the state are now unique in America. Back in the 1970s, when the Pennsylvania Fish and Boat Commission became responsible for managing reptile populations, the state made it illegal to kill rattlesnakes during a roundup.

So now, all Pennsylvania rattlesnake roundups are catch and release: snakes must be captured without the use of toxic chemicals, and regulations say they must be returned to the location in the woods from which they were taken. Also, snake hunters are limited to the taking of a single individual from each of the venomous species present in the state (timber rattlesnakes and copperheads). For the snake hunters, the sport is in seeing who can bring back the longest and heaviest snake. As with roundups in other locations, Pennsylvania roundups are also festivals; often they are fundraisers for a fire company or other community cause.

At first blush, Pennsylvania's approach seems much less harmful than the traditional roundup—after all, no snakes are killed outright. Advocates say the roundups are educational and help people to learn about snakes. But with cash prizes at stake, hunters may be tempted to get a jump on the competition and go after snakes *before* the hunting season legally opens in summer, taking snakes from their dens in winter or spring. Research shows a snake that's disturbed while hibernating may later abandon the area.

Also, though state regulations require hunters to return snakes to the exact location in the woods from which they were taken, it's obviously impossible to enforce this rule. Hunters have to trek up rocky hillsides to collect the snakes; no one knows if how many of them actually make the arduous trudge to carefully return each snake to its specific territory after the roundups.

Yet research increasingly suggests that venomous snakes have very strong ties to their home territories. If released at random, in an unfamiliar location in the woods, a snake often can't find food or shelter and its chances of survival are slim.

Finally, though timber rattlesnakes are not yet a protected species in the state, they are proposed for listing as threatened. As a result, the state does not allow rattlesnake roundups to use this species for the traditional sacking contests, where handlers compete to see who can stuff snakes in a bag the fastest. So, Pennsylvania roundups bring in western diamondbacks for these events. The western snakes are generally captives—they are not returned to the wild or killed after the roundups. But they can be roughly handled and injured during the competitions, so humane societies have concerns about this practice.

Conservation Status

Three of the twenty species of venomous snakes in North America are listed at the U.S. state level as endangered. The copperhead is considered endangered in Massachusetts and Iowa. The massasauga is listed as either endangered or threatened in every state where it occurs—and the U.S. Fish and Wildlife Service has currently designated it as a candidate species for listing as threatened at the federal level.

The timber rattlesnake is listed as either endangered or threatened in more than a dozen states. Habitat loss, past bounty hunting, and rattlesnake roundups are all factors contributing to population declines. It's been especially hard for this species to rebound because of its slow reproductive rate. About two-thirds of all timber rattlesnake females do not breed until they are nine or ten years old. They then have just a few offspring per litter, and they give birth only every other year. Mortality rates for the young snakes are very high. Research is under way to see if this species deserves listing at the federal level.

So far, just one venomous snake is on the U.S. federal endangered species list—the New Mexican ridge-nosed rattlesnake *(Crotalus willardi obscurus)*, a subspecies. The reason for this snake's precarious status seems fairly clear to those who have studied it.

Also found in Mexico, this rattlesnake occurs in the United States in just one two-square mile patch of mountainous habitat in the Animas Mountains of New Mexico. Discovered in the 1950s, it's an unusual-looking snake—paler in color and lacking the white facial stripes of the two other subspecies, the Arizona and Chihuahan ridge-nosed rattlesnakes.

Soon after the discovery, collectors started coming to the area and taking away snakes. With such a small population in such a small area, experts think collecting is likely the reason behind the population decline, although habitat loss is probably a contributing factor.

In 1974, the U.S. Fish and Wildlife Service and the owner of the land where the snakes lived signed an agreement restricting collecting; in 1975, the subspecies was listed as threatened at the federal level (it's considered endangered at the state level). Currently, the nonprofit conservation group The Nature Conservancy controls nearly all the land where this species is found in the United States.

5

Species Identification

This chapter includes an illustrated field guide to the nineteen species of land-dwelling venomous snakes of North America. It's important to note that the count of "nineteen species" is approximate—scientists don't agree on exactly how many species of rattlesnakes there are.

The western rattlesnake, *Crotalis viridis,* is a case in point. Some scientists recognize as many as nine subspecies within this species; others feel strongly that some of these subspecies, such as the Grand Canyon rattlesnake and Hopi rattlesnake, are isolated from the other populations, genetically distinctive, and deserve to be considered species in their own right.

In specifying "snakes of North America," this book refers to snakes of the United States and Canada. Of course, Mexico is also part of North America, and many of the snakes mentioned here have ranges that extend south into Mexico; however, Mexico is also home to a number of venomous snakes with ranges that do not extend north into the United States. Those species are not mentioned here.

Types of Venomous Snakes

Venomous snakes in North America fall into two major groups: members of the Elapidae, or coral snake family, and members of the Viperidae, or viper family (rattlesnakes are pit vipers). Of the twenty venomous species in North America, just three are elapid snakes—the eastern coral snake, Arizona coral snake, and yellow-bellied sea snake. Of the seventeen members of the viper family, fifteen are rattlesnakes. The other two are the copperhead and its close relative the cottonmouth.

Identifying Snakes

Taxonomists identify snakes based on a variety of traits, but one that's particularly distinctive is the shape of the male's sexual organ. Obviously, that's not something the average person can really use to identify venomous snakes in the field—you'll want to make an ID from a good, safe distance.

Some tips for field identification follow. Remember that unlike birds, where you can expect that every robin or cardinal you encounter will look pretty much like the picture in the field guide, rattlesnakes are notorious for variability in their color and scale patterns. You might well encounter a snake that looks absolutely nothing like any photograph of say, a timber rattlesnake that you see in this book, and yet that's what it turns out to be.

How do you make a field identification? First, eliminate the impossible. Think about where you are and rule out species that don't live in that geographic location, or elevation, or habitat. For example, if you're in southern California and you see a rattlesnake with a black tail, you might guess, "timber rattlesnake," but timber rattlers don't live in that area. If you're by a river in Georgia and you see a snake that seems to match the picture for copperhead swim by—well, that's the wrong habitat for a copperhead. It's more likely a juvenile cottonmouth, which looks like a copperhead.

Once you have ruled out the impossible, consider the possibilities, and see which field marks match up with the descriptions provided. Size up the snake: large, medium, or small; slender, average, or stout-bodied. Then start with the obvious, the pattern on the back. Would you describe the snake as striped, spotted, or blotched? What shape are the spots or blotches? Are they round, rectangular, X-shaped, V-shaped, smooth-edged, or irregular? Are they solid colored? Dark with a light border? Dark with a light center?

Next, try to get look at the tail: Does it have a rattle? Is it black? Is it ringed? Are the rings black and white, black and gray, or are they the same colors as the rest of the snake's body? Are the rings of equal or different widths? All of these factors are clues to making the identification.

Finally, take a good look at the head. Does it seem unusually large compared to the body? The same size? Disproportionately small? What color is the face? The top of the head? What size are the scales on the top of the head? Are there any facial marks such as light or dark stripes? Are the pupils round or vertical?

You might make a habit of carrying a camera when you're walking in the woods. If you see a snake, snap a photo—using the zoom function is safer than leaning in closer for a better look. Then you can check for field marks at your leisure, and even show the image to an expert later.

How do you find an expert on snakes? Your local college or university may have a herpetologist (reptile and amphibian expert) on staff; or check with a nature center, state park, science museum, or exploratorium. A wildlife rehabilitator or animal control expert may be willing to field a few questions. Or check to see if your city or state hosts a herpetological society, a club for reptile enthusiasts.

Species Accounts

Each snake species in the field guide section of this book is identified by both a common name and a two-part scientific name (which is Greek or Latin, or both).

Common names are the names we use in everyday speech, names like "eastern diamondback rattlesnake" or "gopher snake." In the United States, the common names that we assign to plants and animals are in English, but in other nations, obviously, common names for snakes and other living things will be in the language of the land.

Although the common name varies with location, the scientific name for each living thing is the same in every nation the world over. This standardization is a way of making sure that scientists who want to compare scholarly notes on, say, the sidewinder and the *víbora de cuernitos* really are talking about the same organism.

Another reason scientific names are useful? Often, over time, a species will accumulate a number of common names. Just look at the cottonmouth, also known as the water moccasin. The average person might start to wonder whether perhaps those are two different snakes. But scientists take a look at the list of identifying features and the scientific name, and they know cottonmouth and water moccasin are one and the same.

Scientific names are always made up of two words. The first word is always capitalized, while the second word is always lowercased. The first word identifies the genus—it places the snake within a group of closely related species. The second word is the species designation—it assigns the snake to a unique species. The Swedish biologist Carl Linnaeus developed this two-part scientific naming system back in the eighteenth century.

The species is the basic unit of biological classification. In general, a species is a group of organisms that share a unique set of characteristics. They look alike, sound alike, and act alike. Members of the same species can mate with one another, and when they do their offspring will be healthy and able to mate with one another.

Members of different species do sometimes mate (hybridize)—for example, a horse and a donkey can mate, and have offspring. But the offspring created when two different species mate (in this case a mule)—will be sterile, unable to produce more offspring.

In studying venomous snakes, you have it easy. You only have to learn the names of a few genera: two in the Elapidae and three in the Viperidae.

Arizona Coral Snake
(*Micruroides euryxanthus*)

Coral Snake Family
(Elapidae)

About the name: The genus name, *Micruroides,* comes from the Greek words *mikros,* meaning "small," and *oura,* meaning "tail," an apt description for a slender snake. The suffix *oides* means "similar to"—specifically, similar to *Micrurus,* the eastern coral snake. The species name, *euryxanthus,* also comes from the Greek: *eurys,* "wide," and *xanthos,* "yellow." The yellow bands around this snake's body may not seem that wide, but compared to an eastern coral snake's narrow yellow bands, they're pretty robust. Found in the Sonoran Desert, this is sometimes called the Sonoran coral snake. Since it's not found exclusively in Arizona, it's sometimes called the "western" coral snake.

Size: Adults can reach 21 inches in length, but 12 to 18 inches is typical. They're very slim—about as thick around as a pencil.

Description: A very colorful snake. The body is ringed with bright colors: wide bands of red and black, separated by narrower bands of yellow or white. The bands go all the way around the body, with the belly the same color as the back, only paler. The tail is ringed with black and yellow—no red. The head is black from the tip of the blunt snout to just behind the eyes.

Look-alike species: Shovel-nosed snakes and variable sand snakes have red, black, and yellow bands, but the colors aren't the same arrangement and intensity. The Arizona mountain kingsnake looks a lot like this coral snake but has a yellow (not black) snout, and the color bands are arranged in a different order: The red and yellow bands are separated by narrow black bands. Remember the rhyme: "Red touch black, venom lack."

Distribution: As its name suggests, this snake is found in Arizona (the central and southern parts). Its range also extends to the southwestern corner of New Mexico and south to western Mexico.

Habitat: Arizona coral snakes live in a variety of dry habitats, including creosote flats, thorn-scrub deserts, oak woodlands, and grasslands, at elevations from sea level to almost 6,000 feet. You often find them snuggled under rocks or discarded lumber in dry, open areas, especially arroyos and river bottoms; they have even been discovered inside buildings.

Feeding habits: Arizona coral snakes specialize in eating blind snakes (very small, thin, wormlike snakes with smooth scales that burrow into loose soil). They also take other small snakes and small lizards. They hunt most actively at night, but will also hunt by day if it's cloudy. Since it takes time for their venom to work, coral snakes tend to hold on to their prey after striking, in contrast to rattlesnakes, which strike and let go.

Distinctive behaviors: Mostly nocturnal, but they may hunt by day in spring and fall. They seem to be more active after it rains. They hibernate underground in cold weather. Arizona coral snakes have an unusual defensive display. A snake threatened by a predator will bury its head in its coils, then raise the tip of its tail and wave it around, like a fake head. At the same time the snake turns the lining of the cloaca (the anal area) inside out, which makes a sharp popping sound. Scientists aren't sure exactly why the snake does this—but it does seem likely to startle an approaching predator.

Breeding habits: Little is known. Snakes are thought to mate in the spring, then females lay two or three eggs in late summer, during the rainy season, The eggs incubate underground, under a rock or a rotting log. After ten weeks, the 7- to 8-inch-long young snakes hatch out.

Eastern Coral Snake *(Micrurus fulvius)*
Texas Coral Snake *(Micrurus tener)*

Coral Snake Family
(Elapidae)

Note: Taxonomists recently confirmed that the Texas coral snake is a unique species, not a subspecies of the eastern coral snake. Since the two species are quite similar, however, they are presented together.

About the name: The genus name of the eastern coral snake, *Micrurus,* comes from the Greek words *mikros,* meaning "small," and *oura,* meaning "tail." The species name, *fulvius,* is from the Latin *fulvus,* meaning orange-yellow in color. The scientist who assigned the name was probably looking at a preserved specimen in which the red rings had faded to a tawny yellow. It's the eastern coral snake because it's found in the eastern half of the United States. Folks also call it the "harlequin snake" or "candy cane snake," for the bright colors.

Size: Adult are usually 20 to 22 inches long. Exceptional specimens can be 4 feet long (twice as long as the Arizona coral snake).

Description: Like its western relative, this coral snake has wide bands of red and black circling the body, with narrow yellow bands between. Usually, the red bands are marked with black spots. The head is black from the tip of snout to just behind eyes, where there's a yellow band.

Look-alike species: The scarlet kingsnake and scarlet snake are similarly striped with red, yellow, and black. (But "red touch black, venom lack.") Also, kingsnakes and scarlet snakes have red noses, not black.

Distribution: This is really more of a "southeastern" coral snake than an "eastern" one. It's found from eastern North Carolina south to Florida and coastal Alabama and Mississippi. The Texas coral snake is found from the western half of Louisiana west to southern Texas. The range extends south into northeastern Mexico.

Habitat: Dry habitat is the key. You'll often find eastern coral snakes in hammocks (elevated, forested mounds). They also live in dry hardwood forests and piney woods, and various scrubby and brushy habitats. Coral snakes are secretive. They spend most of their time under cover, burrowing in sandy soil, or hiding under debris, dead leaves, or downed logs.

Feeding habits: A variety of small lizards make up the bulk of the diet, along with small snakes, including other coral snakes. Very occasionally it takes small birds, lizards, frogs, and insects. The eastern coral snake is not a "sit and wait" hunter; instead, it ferrets out prey quite actively, poking its head under dead leaves or testing the air in underground tunnels. After it strikes, it holds on and chews to make sure a good dose of venom sinks in.

Distinctive behaviors: Eastern coral snakes have a reputation as nocturnal, but scientists who have studied them find they hunt actively by day. They respond to threats by diving into underground burrows or wriggling under leaf litter or debris. If a snake can't hide, it will flatten its body with its head tucked under a coil, then raise its tail and wave it around, attracting the attacker to the least vulnerable part of its body. That leaves the snake free to whip out the real head and bite.

Breeding habits: A flurry of mating in the spring, and then again in the fall. This is such a solitary species that even during mating season, males and females may get aggressive when they see each other. Eventually, though, a male will court a female by slowly rubbing his head and body along her body. She signals her readiness by raising her tail. The eastern coral snake's eggs are more elongated than are most snakes'. They're laid in late spring, in clutches of two to thirteen (four to seven is typical), in leaf litter or underground hollows or under a log—anywhere they will stay moist and be well protected. With no further care from her, they hatch after ninety days, in September. The 7- to 9-inch-long young snakes are fully equipped with venom and ready to hunt for themselves.

Copperhead
(Agkistrodon contortrix)

Viper Family
(Viperidae)

About the name: The genus name comes from the Greek words *ankistron,* which means "fish-hook," and *odontos,* which means "tooth"—a perfect description of the copperhead's sharp fangs. The species name, *contortrix,* is Latin for "contortionist," possibly describing the twisty pattern on the back, or maybe the contorted specimen the taxonomist happened to examine. The common name describes this species' most distinctive feature, its copper-colored head. The copperhead's close relative, the cottonmouth, is known as the "water moccasin," so some rural folks call the upland-dwelling copperhead the "highland moccasin."

Size: Though stout-bodied, copperheads are more slender than most pit vipers. Adults are usually about 2 feet long, but larger snakes are common. The longest known copperhead measured 53 inches.

Description: The distinctive copper-colored head is triangular and much wider than the neck. The basic body color is earth-toned, anything from tan to light brown to pinkish. This background is overlaid with X-shaped or hourglass-shaped crossbands that can be dark brown to reddish brown in color. Juvenile copperheads look like mini-adults, except that the tips of their tails are bright yellow.

Look-alike species: The mottled color patterns of corn snake, water snake, and eastern hognose snake shout "copperhead" to the inexperienced observer, but these species have patterned (not solid-colored) heads and lack the distinctive viper facial pit and vertical pupils. The western lyre snake is also similar in color and pattern to the copperhead and even has vertical pupils, but it has a patterned head.

Distribution: This is an eastern species. You'll find copperheads from southwestern Massachusetts west to Nebraska and south to northern Florida and west Texas.

Habitat: Copperheads live in a variety of habitats, from rocky outcrops on wooded hillsides to mixed hardwood and pine forests to swamp edges. As long as there's plenty of ground cover in the form of tangled vegetation, old vines, or rotting logs, a copperhead is happy. The wood-toned scale pattern helps this species blend in with a carpet of dead leaves. In summer months, copperheads seek out wet areas near streams and creeks.

Feeding habits: Some venomous snakes specialize, but copperheads take a variety of prey. Adults eat mostly vertebrates: small rodents, lizards, frogs, toads, salamanders, and other snakes. But they'll also take the largest insects such as cicadas, grasshoppers, and beetles. Young snakes use their yellow tail tips like fishing lures—they wiggle them to attract lizards and frogs. Copperheads are usually ambush predators, but they sometimes pursue their prey and will even climb trees after cicadas. With large prey items, such as a rodent, the snake will strike and release, then follow the odor trail. With smaller prey such as frogs and birds, the snake strikes and holds the prey until the venom takes effect.

Distinctive behaviors: On cool days in spring and fall, you may spot a copperhead basking in the sun; once they warm up, they hunt during the day. In summer, they're more active in the cool of the night. In fall, copperheads head for their dens, usually holes in rocky outcrops, on hillsides with a sunny southern or eastern exposure, then hibernate over the winter. Several copperheads will share one den site, which may also be occupied by other species, including black rat snakes or timber rattlesnakes. Each snake returns to the same den every year.

Breeding habits: Most mating activity happens in the spring, but it can also take place in the fall, since the female can store sperm. A male snake will follow the female's pheromone trail, then court her by touching her with his snout and rubbing her neck with his chin. Two males who cross paths may engage in ritualized combat. Gestation lasts 105 to 150 days, and the young are born in August to October, typically four to eight per litter. A female has a litter only every other year, unless food is plentiful.

Cottonmouth
(Agkistrodon piscivorous)

Viper Family
(Viperidae)

About the name: This member of the genus *Agkistrodon* earned the species name *piscivorous* for its fish-eating habits. *Piscis* is Latin for "fish," and *voro* is Latin for "to devour." Many people refer to this snake as the water moccasin or cottonmouth moccasin. It's called a cottonmouth because the lining of its mouth is white—something you tend to notice because, if this snake feels threatened, it will stand its ground and open its mouth wide, like a snarling dog or cat. (The white mouth lining is unusual; most snakes have red or black inside the mouth.)

Size: Typically 3 to 4 feet long, but the largest recorded specimen was more than 6 feet long.

Description: These heavy-bodied snakes are dark overall in color, olive-green to brown to black. The western subspecies is darker than the eastern subspecies. Look closely—within that dark color, there's usually a pattern of dark-on-dark crossbands that are most visible on the sides. But big snakes may be solid black, not banded. The belly has dirty yellow-and-brown blotches. The head is broad at the base, noticeably wider than the neck, and flat topped. Some snakes have a dark brown cheek stripe with light borders. Young cottonmouths look a lot like copperheads, their close relatives; they are lighter in color than they will be as adults, and their crossbands tend to be more visible. Like juvenile copperheads, they have bright yellow or greenish tail tips.

Look-alike species: Nonvenomous water snakes look similar and are found in the same habitat; however, they lack the distinctive viper facial pits and vertical pupils. Also, they swim with just the head and neck above the water, whereas the cottonmouth inflates its one lung so that most of its body floats on the surface when it swims.

Distribution: This snake is found throughout most of the southeastern United States—along the East Coast from Virginia to the upper Florida Keys, and west to southern Illinois, southern Missouri, south-central Oklahoma, and central Texas.

Habitat: Found mostly in swamps or marshes—always close to some body of water, whether it's a lake, pond, river, stream, slough, canal, or rice field.

Feeding habits: These are opportunistic predators that will ambush prey, forage actively, and even scavenge. Known prey items include fish, small mammals, birds, lizards, frogs, salamanders, small turtles, other snakes, and even baby alligators. Cottonmouths tend to strike and hold their prey. Young cottonmouths, like young copperheads, use their colorful tails as lures to attract frogs.

Distinctive behaviors: Cottonmouths spend almost all their time in or close to water. They have a reputation as aggressive snakes that will stand their ground when disturbed, hissing aggressively and gaping to show the white "cottonmouth." They are good climbers and often work their way onto low tree branches hanging over the water so they can bask in the sun.

Breeding habits: Males find females by following their pheromone trails. The males sometimes engage in ritual combat, which can take place in the water as well as on land. Cottonmouths probably do most of their mating in the spring, but researchers have documented mating in all times of the year. The females probably store sperm since the young are usually born alive in August or September. Litters can include from one to twenty young (seven is typical) that are 7 to 13 inches long at birth. Females don't breed until they are three years old, and then they usually bear young only every other year or every third year.

Massasauga
(Sistrurus catenatus)

Viper Family
(Viperidae)

About the name: There are two rattlesnake genera; *Crotalus* gets its name from the Greek word for "rattle." Taxonomists were not terribly inventive; they named the genus *Sistrurus* for the Latin word for rattle, *sistrum,* combined with the Greek word for tail, *oura.* The real-life sistrum was a tamborinelike instrument that Egyptian women used when worshipping the goddess Isis. Squint a little, and with its oval shape and crossbars, the sistrum resemble a rattlesnake's rattle. Massasauga is the Ojibwe Indian word for "great river mouth." These snakes do like damp environments (some call them "swamp rattlesnakes"), but massasauga is also a name given to many geographic features in the snake's range.

Size: This is a smallish but stout rattlesnake, typically 1 1/2 to, at most, 3 feet long.

Description: The background color is gray to light brown overall, but massasaugas have a complex pattern on top of that. First, there's a row of prominent dark (brown to black), often rectangular spots marching down the back. Then there are three more rows of dark spots on each side of the body. The spots turn into dark rings at the tail end. (Once in a while you see an individual snake that's striped all over instead of spotted.) The Arizona population is reddish in color. Notice the dark stripe on the head that runs from the eye down past the angle of the jaw. Also, on top of the head, between and in front of the eyes, instead of small scales there are nine noticeable large scales.

Look-alike species: Nonvenomous species such as the fox snake, water snake, hognose snake, and Great Plains rat snake can have similarly complex patterns but lack the viper traits of facial pit and vertical pupil, and, of course, have no rattles. The pygmy rattlesnake is smaller and more pale in color. The larger *Crotalus* rattlesnakes have small scales on the top of the head, not large ones.

Distribution: This species' range is unusual—it's not primarily eastern or western, but distributed in a wide diagonal stripe across the United States, from western New York to west Texas, and continuing into southern New Mexico and southeastern Arizona.

Habitat: Likes wet, lowland areas, including swamps, marshes, bogs, and wet meadows. In the arid southwestern states, you find it along river bottoms and in dry grasslands where it uses rodent burrows as cool, humid retreats.

Feeding habits: Massasaugas take a lot of small rodents, mostly voles, along with deer mice. Also on the menu: small snakes such as garter snakes, other small rodents, and the occasional grassland bird. Massasaugas in desert habitats take lizards, while snakes in wetter habitats take frogs, toads, crayfish, and even small fish. Young snakes use their tails as lures to attract frogs.

Distinctive behaviors: Massasaugas can always be found close to, but not directly next to, water such as a marsh, a lake, or river. They spend their days quietly hanging out in a convenient tuft of grass or under a rock or a brush pile. Most rattlesnakes hibernate in groups but massasaugas go solo, curling up in rodent burrows or, most often, in crayfish burrows and rock piles. In spring, as the water rises in creeks and marshes, they move from their burrows to drier, upland habitat. During the rest of the year these snakes are usually active by day, but in summer if temperatures get very hot, they'll switch to hunting at night, when temperatures are cooler. As you might expect from a snake that lives near water, they are good swimmers.

Breeding habits: Females breed for the first time at the age of three. Scientists aren't sure when breeding season is; possibly spring, but probably late summer and fall. The female stores sperm over the winter. After a gestation period of about 100 to 115 days the young are born alive in late summer. A litter can be two to nineteen young, but eight to ten is usual. Young snakes are 5 to 7 inches long when born and have a yellow tail tip.

Pygmy Rattlesnake
(Sistrurus miliarius)

Viper Family
(Viperidae)

About the name: The species name, *miliarius,* is Latin for "milletlike." Millet is a grain that grows in long "sprays" or tails packed with tiny seeds that resemble the scales on a snake. The common name is apt, since this snake is so tiny. Some people call them "buzzworms," for their small size and faint rattle. Another nickname is "ground-rattler." Researchers affectionately call them "pigs."

Size: The biggest adults are a mere 18 inches long. Coiled on the forest floor, a snake takes up about as much space as a big pinecone.

Description: Compared to the closely related massasauga, this small snake has a more star-spangled or polka-dot appearance. Against a gray to tan background, a row of irregular dark brown to black blotches runs down the back; there are one to three more rows of side spots. A red to orange stripe down the middle of the back adds color. Another distinctive touch is the thick black or reddish brown stripe that runs from the corner of each eye back beyond the corner of the mouth. Also, on top of the head, instead of small scales, there are nine noticeably large scales.

Look-alike species: The eastern hognose snake is variable in appearance; spotted individuals could be confused with this species, although hognose snakes lack the rattle and facial pit of rattlesnakes and have round, not vertical, pupils. The massasauga tends to be larger and darker in color; other rattlesnakes in the genus *Crotalus* are significantly larger and have small (not large) scales on the head.

Distribution: This snake's home range is from North Carolina south to the Florida Keys and west to eastern Oklahoma and central Texas.

Habitat: In the East, you can find this little snake in forest habitats, but always close to some body of water. In southern regions, where gopher tortoises live, this species will often use a tortoise burrow as a retreat. In the westernmost part of its range, in Texas and Oklahoma, the pygmy rattlesnake makes a home in grasslands, but only areas that don't get too dried out.

Feeding habits: Pygmy rattlesnakes are ambush predators that take a variety of prey, all of it appropriate for their small size: *Anolis* lizards and tree frogs or leopard frogs, insects, spiders, centipedes, toads, other small snakes, nestlings, and mice.

Distinctive behaviors: These snakes are active all year round in the south, but in North Carolina they may hibernate from December through February. They tend to occupy a small home range and not move very far. The tiny rattle is hard to hear. Scientists conjecture the tail is used more for luring prey than for threat displays.

Breeding habits: Females are ready to breed at just two years of age and sometimes can breed two years in a row. Males engage in combat dances to establish dominance. Mating takes place in the fall; a male will stay with and guard a female for days at a time. Females store sperm over the winter for spring fertilization, then the young are born alive in late summer. In contrast to most rattlesnakes, the females do feed while gestating. The newborn snakes are so tiny, a coiled snake would fit on a half-dollar coin. The litter size ranges from two to twelve (seven to ten is typical).

Eastern Diamondback Rattlesnake
(Crotalus adamanteus)

Viper Family
(Viperidae)

About the name: The genus name *Crotalus* comes from the Greek word *krotalon,* meaning a rattle, a reference to the anatomical structure that makes this group of snakes unique. The species name, *adamanteus,* is derived from the Latin word for diamond, *adamantis,* which is itself derived from a Greek word, *adamantos,* meaning "hard steel," since diamonds, like steel, are very hard, with a cutting edge. It's the "eastern" diamondback because it's found in the East and has a pattern of diamonds down its back.

Size: This is the largest venomous snake in North America—and the largest rattlesnake in the world. A typical adult is 4 feet long and weighs 4 or 5 pounds, but 8-footers have been collected; snakes this size could weigh as much as 50 pounds.

Description: This is a very heavy-bodied snake. The large head is set off from the body by a narrow neck. A line of diamonds—dark brown shading to pale in the middle, and outlined in pale yellow—marches down the spine. The head is marked on each side by two light-colored diagonal lines, one in front of the eye and one behind, giving the snake a "masked bandit" appearance. The tail is ringed in brown and white.

Look-alike species: No other rattlesnake in the eastern United States resembles this one. The diamond back, white facial stripes, and ringed tail are all distinctive.

Distribution: This is a southern species with a limited distribution, from coastal North Carolina south to the Florida Keys then west to southern Mississippi and eastern Louisiana.

Habitat: Most of the snake's original habitat—longleaf pine forests—has been logged off, so diamondbacks have moved into other habitat: loblolly pine and turkey oak forests, dry pine flatwoods, vacant lots, and abandoned farmlands. They're generally found at lower elevations, from sea level to about 500 feet. In areas where gopher tortoises are present, diamondbacks frequently hang out in their burrows, roomy underground refuges that are often as much as 6 feet deep.

Feeding habits: Adults eat good-sized small mammals such as rabbits, but will also take squirrels, rice rats, and occasionally birds. (Four or five rabbits a year is enough calories for a big adult snake.) Young snakes take smaller mammals such as mice. These are ambush predators. A diamondback will coil up under a clump of grass or palmetto and wait for as long as a week until a mouse or rat wanders by. After the strike it releases its prey to die, then tracks it down.

Distinctive behaviors: In the northern parts of their range, eastern diamondbacks go underground for the winter, in gopher tortoise burrows, hollow stumps, armadillo holes, or the root channels under saw palmetto thickets. They do come out to bask on warm days, however. Diamondbacks are good swimmers. They will tackle both fresh and saltwater, and have been spotted on coastal islands, miles from shore.

Breeding habits: Not much is known. It's thought that mating happens both in spring and fall. Gestation last six to seven months. The young are born alive between July and early October; seven to twenty-one in a litter (twelve is typical), measuring 12 to 15 inches long.

Western Diamondback Rattlesnake
(*Crotalus atrox*)

Viper Family
(Viperidae)

About the name: The species name, *atrox,* is Latin for "fierce" or "savage," and indeed this species has a reputation for being easily irritated and quick to strike. It's the "western" diamondback because it's found in western states, as opposed to the eastern diamondback, found east of the Mississippi. Black and white rings on the tail earn it the nickname "coontail."

Size: Only the eastern diamondback is larger. Typical adults are 1 to 4 feet long, but individuals often reach well over 6 feet in length.

Description: This snake is very heavy bodied. The background color and pattern are quite variable, usually matching the habitat in which the snake lives, but, in general, the background is light-gray to light brown—which sets off the dark, diamond-shaped blotches that run down the back. Usually each diamond has a light (yellow or cream-colored) border. Smaller dark blotches mark the sides. The tail is distinctly ringed in gray or white and black. Each side of the face is marked with a pair of light stripes that run from the mouth to the eyes.

Look-alike species: The northern Mojave rattlesnake looks similar, but check the tail—the white tail bands are twice as wide as the black bands; in the western diamondback they are equal in width. The red diamond rattlesnake has an almost identical scale pattern but is redder in color. Gopher snakes, hognose snakes, rat snakes, and copperheads have patterned backs and perform a similar threat display, but look closely: no rattle.

Distribution: This snake is found in the southwestern corner of the United States, from southeastern California and southern Nevada through southern Arizona and southern New Mexico to Texas, south-central Oklahoma, and western Arkansas. Its range also extends southward in Mexico to northeastern Baja California.

Habitat: This is a foothills, not a mountain, species found mostly at fairly low elevations. It's considered a habitat generalist—many different environments are acceptable, as long as they are dry. You can find western diamondbacks in desert, dry grasslands, scrub-oak juniper forests, thorn scrub-lands, open conifer forests, even curled under debris in rural junkyards. Within all these habitats, diamondbacks hang out where there are rocky outcrops or boulders, hiding in crevices in the rocks.

Feeding habits: These snakes take a wide variety of prey but seem to prefer small mammals such as shrews, mice and rats, cottontail rabbits, and squirrels. In lab tests, they even ate carrion. They usually hunt at night, locating their prey by infrared reception or by smell, feeding every two to three weeks. Although their venom is certainly powerful enough to kill the prey, scientists conjecture that small animals are actually done in by the extra-long fangs.

Distinctive behaviors: Disturb a western diamondback and it will hold its ground, raising its head and tail high as it hisses and rattles. This species hibernates in winter, though on warm winter days it will emerge from the den to bask in the sun. Hibernation sites may be caves on south-facing slopes or animal burrows, often prairie dog burrows in grassland habitats. As many as a hundred snakes will congregate in one den for hibernation, and sometimes other snake species join them. Like the timber rattlesnake, this species makes fairly lengthy annual migrations (more than a mile) between its summer feeding grounds and winter den.

Breeding habits: Males compete in ritual combat. Mating can take place both in spring and fall. Scientists aren't sure but think females don't reproduce until they are three years old. Then they bear young every other year. The young are born alive in late summer to early fall. A typical litter is about ten offspring (the range is nine to fourteen), although snakes in drier environments seem to have fewer young. The young snakes measure 9 to 13 inches long.

Sidewinder
(Crotalus cerastes)

Viper Family
(Viperidae)

About the name: The species name, *cerastes,* comes from the Greek word "kerastes," which means "horned." The pointed scales that stick out above the eyes like little horns give this snake a wicked appearance; some people call it the horned rattlesnake. It's called the sidewinder for the unusual way it moves, by looping sideways.

Size: This is a small snake. Adults are rarely more than 2 feet long.

Description: Sidewiders are pale overall. The background color is the color of sand: gray, tan, cream, or pale pink. A series of spots runs the length of the back; they're usually reddish brown but can range in color from dark tan to yellow-brown through orange to gray. The head is marked by a dark stripe with a light border that runs from the eye to the corner of the mouth. The short tail is dark brown or black. Some observers say females tend to be larger than males.

For years scientists wondered why sidewinders had horns. One idea was that the horns were a built-in sunshade, like the brim of a baseball cap, protecting the snake's eyes from the glare of the desert sun. But this snake is mostly active at night. Anyway, daytime observations suggest the scales do little to shade the eyes.

Another idea was that the scales folded down to protect the snakes' eyes from scratchy sand when it was tunneling underground. In the late 1960s, scientists observing captive snakes discovered that the snakes themselves can fold down their scales when moving about in tight quarters, so it's likely the scales do serve as sand goggles underground.

Look-alike species: None. This is the only snake in the southwestern United States with little horns over its eyes.

Distribution: In the United States, this species is found in the Mojave and Sonoran Deserts, in a four-state area that includes extreme southwestern Utah, southern Nevada, southeastern California, and southwestern Arizona. Its range also extends southward into northwestern Sonora, eastern Baja California, and Isla Tiburon in Mexico.

Habitat: This snake is found only in the most arid lowland deserts, usually below 5,000 feet, in areas with little or no plant life, anything from loose sandy washes to hard pan flats and rocky areas.

Feeding habits: The most nocturnal of the rattlesnakes, sidewinders mostly take small rodents and lizards. Their most common prey are desert-dwelling pocket mice and kangaroo rats. They are ambush predators and will wait patiently outside a rodent or lizard burrow, partially concealed in the sand, until the occupant emerges under what it thinks is the cover of darkness.

Distinctive behaviors: This snake's most distinctive behavior is its favored mode of locomotion—sidewinding—a way to conserve energy when moving over loose sand (sidewinders *are* capable of moving in other ways, including the undulation typical of most rattlesnakes). In the northernmost part of their range, sidewinders hibernate from October through March, usually in rodent burrows. In summer, a snake will avoid the extreme daytime heat by hiding out in an animal burrow or coiling up and edging its way under a blanket of sand in the shade of a bush. At night, as temperatures drop rapidly, sidewinders often crawl onto still-hot asphalt roads to warm up; as a result, they're all-too-often run over by cars.

Breeding habits: Mating has been observed in the spring and in the fall. Young are born alive in the fall; a litter can be from five to eighteen young but is typically seven to twelve snakes, 6 to 8 inches long.

Timber and Canebrake Rattlesnake
(Crotalus horridus)

Viper Family
(Viperidae)

About the name: The genus name, *horridus,* scarcely needs explanation, but in case it does, it's based on the Latin word for "dreadful." In wooded, mountainous northern areas, locals call them timber rattlesnakes; people in the South and on the coastal plain, however, call them canebrake rattlesnakes, after the dense stands of canebrake bamboo common where snakes are found.

Size: Typically 3 to 4¹/₂ feet long. The longest snake on record measured a little more than 6 feet.

Description: The diamond-shaped head is set off from the body by a fairly thin neck. In the Northeast and the Appalachians, these snakes exist in two color phases. Yellow-phase snakes are most common; the background color may be yellowish, light brown, or gray, accented with black or dark-brown, V-shaped crossbands. Black-phase snakes also have dark crossbands, but they're barely visible against a dark background. The tail is a deep black (it's sometimes called a "velvet-tail") with a tan rattle. The canebrake subspecies, found in the southern part of the range, has a distinctive orange or reddish-brown stripe running the length of its back. Young snakes look like adults, except more brightly marked.

Look-alike species: Eastern diamondback, western diamondback, and western rattlesnakes all look similar, and each overlaps with timber rattlesnake in parts of its range, but all have white stripes on the sides of their faces (which this species lacks), a striped (not dark) tail, and diamonds or rectangles down the back (not Vs). Pygmy rattlesnakes and massasaugas are similar but smaller, and they also have distinctive enlarged scales on the top of the head (this species has small scales on the head).

Distribution: Found more or less throughout the entire eastern half of the United States, except the Great Lakes region, most of New York and New England, and Florida. Look for it from southern New Hampshire and southern Ontario south to northern Georgia and west to Minnesota through Texas.

Habitat: In the North, you'll find timber rattlesnakes in oak woodlands in remote, rocky mountain areas. They need two kinds of habitat over the course of the year: high rocky outcrops with southerly exposures for winter denning, and open deciduous forests in the valleys below for summer hunting. In the South, you may find canebrake rattlesnakes on wooded hillsides but also in damp habitats, such as near riverbanks, in swamps, and in namesake canebrake thickets.

Feeding habits: Mostly takes small mammals such as mice, shrews, voles, chipmunks, squirrels, and rabbits, but occasionally take ground-nesting birds and birds' eggs, too. These are classic ambush predators. They'll hang out at the logs that mice use as runways, or wait at the base of a tree, head up, for a squirrel to come down. They strike and release, then follow the dying animal's scent.

Distinctive behaviors: Timber rattlesnakes hibernate in winter—depending on the region and climate, this can be for a few weeks to a few months. In the mountains, snakes hibernate in communal dens, dozens of snakes to a den, sometimes sharing space with copperheads as well as nonvenomous snakes like bullheads, milksnakes, black rat snakes, and racers and the lizards called skinks. In summer, snakes may travel a few miles from the den sites to hunt in nearby forests or lowland meadows. Pregnant females, on the other hand, may stay near the den all summer.

Breeding habits: Timber rattlesnakes are very slow to mature; a female doesn't breed until she is seven to ten years old, and then she bears young only every two or three years. Mating usually takes place in fall. Males engage in ritual combat. Females store sperm over the winter and fertilize their eggs in spring. Gestation takes four to five months and the litter of six to eighteen (nine are typical) is born alive in late summer. Females stay with their young for up to two weeks, until the first time they shed their skin.

Rock Rattlesnake
(Crotalus lepidus)

Viper Family
(Viperidae)

About the name: The species name means neat, graceful, or pleasant. It's not known why this name was chosen for the species, but it is known that the scientist was working with preserved specimens, not live snakes. The rock rattlesnake does tend to hang out in rocky habitat.

Size: This is a modestly sized snake; adults are rarely more than 2 feet long. For their length, however, they have fairly heavy bodies and large heads.

Description: As with many rattlesnakes, populations vary in color and pattern to match their environment. So the background color for a rock rattlesnake may be any shade of gray, tan, or pink: Where the bedrock is volcanic, snakes are dark. Where it's limestone, snakes are light gray. The background color is accented with contrasting dark crossbands (dark brown or black) that may have pale borders. In some populations, the crossbands are distinct and clean-edged, but in others they shatter into patterns of speckles; in some cases the bands are so intricate, snakes look like they are wearing fabulous hand-knit Norwegian sweaters. On the head, a pinkish-brown stripe runs backward from just under the eye to the corner of the mouth.

Look-alike species: The gray-banded kingsnake is found in some of the same areas and has a similar color, but the pupil is round, not vertical, and the kingsnake lacks the rattle and facial pits. As for other banded rattlesnakes, in the rock rattler, the scale just in front of each eye is divided vertically. No other rattlesnake has this feature.

Distribution: This species has a limited distribution in the southwestern United States, from extreme southwestern Texas and southern New Mexico to the corner of southeastern Arizona. It has a much larger distribution in northern Mexico.

Habitat: Rock rattlesnakes live in rocky, dry areas at moderate elevations (2,000 to 7,500 feet) in hilly terrain. You can find them anywhere from mesquite grasslands and brushy habitat up rock-strewn hillsides and through dry arroyos to ponderosa pine forests. They like to hang out in rocky outcrops and in crevices along boulder-strewn slopes, hence the name rock rattlesnakes. Since the twentieth century, man-made road cuts have become another popular habitat.

Feeding habits: Prefers other reptiles, mostly lizards, along with small snakes such as the western hooknose. When they strike at lizards, they tend to hang on to the prey until it's unconscious and ready to be swallowed.

Distinctive behaviors: Has a reputation as a comparatively calm rattlesnake. If it feels threatened, it tends to lie quietly and rely on camouflage to avoid trouble. If hassled, it's more likely to try to slither away to a safe place than coil and strike. More likely to be active at cold temperatures than other rattlesnakes, the rock rattlesnake is out and about year-round in Mexico, but in the northern part of its range it hibernates from December to April, denning up below the frost line, under rocks or tree stumps.

Breeding habits: Rock rattlesnakes take three or more years to become sexually mature. Males engage in ritual combat. They breed in the spring, and the young are usually born alive in late July and August, averaging about four young per litter (the range is one to eight). The young, 7 to 8 inches long, look like tiny adults.

Speckled Rattlesnake
(Crotalus mitchelli)

Viper Family
(Viperidae)

About the name: The species name honors Silas Weir Mitchell (1829–1914), a Philadelphia physician and neurological researcher. At the time the young taxonomist Edward Drinker Cope named this snake for Mitchell, Cope was just twenty-one years old and a student at the University of Pennsylvania. Mitchell was thirty-one and had recently published his landmark paper "Researches on the Venom of the Rattlesnake" through the Smithsonian Institution to wide acclaim. This is the "speckled" rattlesnake because each individual scale is light in color but dotted with tiny, dark speckles.

Size: A typical adult is about 3 to 4 feet long.

Description: Other western rattlesnakes vary in appearance; this is the most variable of all, with members of each population matching the soil of the habitat in which they are found. The background color is light—anything from off-white to gray to yellowish to pink to pale orange to tan to brown. Against this background, small dark spots merge into a kind of folded-over inkblot pattern of blurry crossbands or blotchy diamonds. Overall, the colors appear faded, not bright and fresh like those of a diamondback. The net effect is that many of these snakes look like chunks of well-worn granite. As with many rattlesnakes, the tail is circled with dark rings; however, there are no facial stripes.

Look-alike species: The sidewinder, found in the same areas, has "horns" over its eyes. Other fellow desert dwellers, the western diamondback and Mojave rattlesnake, are more brightly colored.

Distribution: Speckled rattlesnakes occur throughout the Mojave and Sonoran Deserts, which means you find them in southern Nevada, southern California, and western Arizona. Their range also extends south to Baja California Sur and northern Sonora, Mexico. They occur in low to moderate elevations, from about 600 to 7,000 feet.

Habitat: These desert rattlers live in the hottest, driest areas, in zones littered with rocks: canyons, buttes, erosion gullies, and alluvial fans. They're associated with such desert vegetation as sagebrush, creosote, chapparal, pinyon, and juniper.

Feeding habits: Speckled rattlesnakes feed both by active foraging and ambush. They seem to take mostly small mammals: ground squirrels, wood rats, kangaroo rats, and pocket mice are common prey. But they'll also take lizards, and young snakes specialize on them.

Distinctive behaviors: Observers describe this as an alert, nervous species, quick to strike if provoked. Snakes hibernate from late October to April in rock crevices, animal burrows, or abandoned mines. One den may accommodate dozens of snakes. During the summer, speckled rattlesnakes tend to be most active at night; they spend the hottest parts of the day in the shade, coiled under rocks or bushes or hidden in rodent burrows.

Breeding habits: Mating season seems to be from July through September. The young are born alive in late summer to early fall. Litter size can be from two to eleven; four to eight is typical. The young snakes are $8^1/_2$ to $10^1/_2$ inches long.

Black-tailed Rattlesnake
(Crotalus molossus)

Viper Family
(Viperidae)

About the name: The species name comes from the Greek *molossos;* the Molossians were an ancient tribe, regarded by their neighbors as barbarians and known for their vicious molossus hounds, heavy-bodied dogs similar to a mastiff hound. The common name, "black-tailed rattlesnake," describes this snake's distinctive black tail.

Size: About 3 to 4 feet.

Description: This is an unusually beautiful snake. The background color of the body varies from yellow to olive green to brown. Against this background is a pattern of very dark brown or black blotches or crossbands, sometimes diamond shaped, that have jagged edges. The irregular edges give the snake a tapestried appearance, like a bit of Navajo carpet. It also has a solid black tail, and often a black snout, so it looks like it's wearing a bandit's mask. You find the darkest snakes in areas where the soil and rocks are dark in color.

Look-alike species: Nonvenomous snakes within this species' range may have elaborately patterned backs but lack a rattle. Of the other rattlesnakes within the same range, only the timber rattlesnake also has a black tail, but these two species overlap only in central Texas.

Distribution: In the United States, the blacktail is found from Arizona east to central Texas. Its range extends south through central Mexico. Isolated populations also live on the Tiburon and San Esteban Islands in the Gulf of California. This snake can occur at elevations from sea level to about 9,500 feet.

Habitat: Within upland forests, snakes find a home at rocky sites such as rockslides, rock outcrops, rimrock, and dry streambeds. At lower elevations, in habitats such as mesquite grasslands and chapparal, they're often found in arroyos.

Feeding habits: Blacktails switch from hunting in morning and late afternoon during the cool weather of spring and fall to nocturnal hunting during hot summer weather. This is mainly an ambush hunter that strikes and releases prey, then follows the odor trail. Its main prey are small mammals such as mice, woodrats, and ground squirrels, but it will take the occasional bird or lizard.

Distinctive behaviors: Quick to rattle when disturbed, the black-tailed rattlesnake tends to give away its hiding place. Hibernation dates vary with location and the severity of winter weather; the snakes use rodent burrows, holes and crevices in rock piles, and caves as den sites. In summer, they hunt by day but may shift to night hunting pattern if weather is very hot. This snake is good at climbing trees and rock piles, and even though it's a desert dweller, it also swims well. It's also good at sidewinding.

Breeding habits: Males engage in ritual combat, and the male stays with the female for several weeks after mating. The young are born alive in late summer. Litters range in size from three to sixteen young, which average 7 to 12 inches long at birth. Females may be able to breed every year if conditions are good.

Twin-spotted Rattlesnake
(Crotalus pricei)

Viper Family
(Viperidae)

About the name: California herpetologist Van Denburgh gave this snake the species name *pricei* to honor the natural history enthusiast William Wightman Price (1871–1922), who collected a specimen of this snake, previously unknown to science, while a student at Stanford University. The common name describes the neat double rows of dark spots that parade down the back, giving this rattlesnake a distinctive appearance.

Size: A small, slender snake, rarely more than 2 feet long.

Description: The background color is usually blue-gray or pale brown—but occasionally reddish snakes are seen. The pattern on the back consists of pairs of dark spots (either brown or black). On some snakes, the spots alternate (they're positioned on the diagonal); on some snakes, the spots are side by side, and near the tail the spots merge into crossbands. There can also be smaller dark spots on the sides. The segment of the rattle closest to the tail is orange or red. On the face, there's often a dark stripe that extends from below the eye back along the cheek.

Look-alike species: The ridge-nosed rattlesnake is similar but has an upturned snout, and the pattern on its back includes white crossbars. The rock rattlesnake could also be confused for this species, but usually its dark blotches form bars, not spots, and it lacks the dark cheek stripe.

Distribution: This species has a particularly limited distribution in the United States (it's mainly a Mexican species). It's found only in southeastern Arizona, and only in five isolated populations, on so-called "sky islands," isolated mountaintops separated from each other by an ocean of lowland habitat inhospitable to these snakes. The specific places where you find twin-spotted rattlers are the Chiricahua, Pinaleño, Huachuca, and Santa Rita mountain ranges.

Habitat: As you might expect from its limited distribution, the twin-spot is a habitat specialist—a mountain dweller that favors tumbled piles of rocks on steep slopes nested in canyons of pine-oak or conifers at fairly high altitudes, from 6,000 to 11,000 feet.

Feeding habits: Spiny lizards are this snake's most common prey, but it will take the occasional small mammal or even a fellow rattlesnake, and some populations catch a good number of nestling birds. Unlike most other small rattlesnakes, this species is not known to use its tail as a lure.

Distinctive behavior: Observers say this is a shy snake that will crawl away rather than strike. The rattle is so soft, you could mistake it for the buzz of some summer insect.

Breeding habits: It's thought this species mates in August or September and stores sperm over the winter. The young are born alive in July or August. Litters can be from three to nine young but five to six is typical. The females bear young every other year, or less often.

Red Diamond Rattlesnake
(Crotalus ruber)

Viper Family
(Viperidae)

About the name: The species name, *ruber,* is from the Latin for "red," a reference to its overall reddish color. Like the eastern and western diamondbacks, it has diamonds down the length of its back.

Size: These tend to be pretty big snakes. Adults are typically 4 to 5 feet long. The record for this species is 5 feet, 5 inches long.

Description: The background color is always reddish: brick red, reddish gray, or pinkish brown. The marks down the back are diamond shaped with light borders. Other rattlesnake species tend to match the color of the soil in their habitat, but in this species, individuals within a population may vary in color. The tail is thick and ringed with black and gray or black and white; males have thicker tails than females. The head is marked with two light diagonal stripes.

Look-alike species: This attractive snake looks a lot like a western diamondback rattlesnake, if the western diamondback had a red color phase (it does not). You're not likely to confuse the two, however, since their ranges overlap only in a small area in California.

Distribution: In the United States, the red diamond rattlesnake is found only in a small area in southern California, from San Bernardino and Los Angeles Counties southward to the border with Mexico. In Mexico, you can find it as far south as Cabo San Lucas in Baja California, and also on several islands in the Gulf of California, as well as Isla de Santa Margarita in the Pacific Ocean.

Habitat: Red diamond rattlesnakes live at elevations from sea level to about 5,000 feet, either in rocky areas or in areas with dense vegetation such as chaparral, thorn-scrub, or pine-oak woods.

Feeding habits: This ambush hunter mostly takes small mammals such as rabbits, ground squirrels, kangaroo rats, and wood rats. Young snakes take smaller prey such as mice and lizards.

Distinctive behaviors: Even though this snake lives close to San Diego, one of the most densely populated urban areas in North America, and even though it's a big snake, it's little studied and rarely observed, so not much is known about its habits. It's considered to be mild mannered for a big snake, the kind of snake that lets you get close without rattling. In the winter, small numbers of snakes will share a den, often a rodent burrow or a crevice between rocks. In the hot summers of southern California, it hunts in the cool of night. A good climber and swimmer, it's been spotted high in cactus branches and swimming across San Diego's reservoirs.

Breeding habits: Males engage in ritual combat. Mating takes place in early spring. Young are born in August and September. A litter can be three to twenty young, but eight to ten is typical. Newborns are not as brightly colored as their parents adults; they are large at birth, averaging 11 to 14 inches long.

Mojave Rattlesnake
(Crotalus scutulatus)

Viper Family
(Viperidae)

About the name: *Scutulatus* is a Latin word that means "having a shield-shaped patch." The large, dark patches that ornament this snake's back do, with some imagination, resemble a chain of heraldic shields. The common name is appropriate, since this snake's home range is centered on the Mojave Desert. In areas where the snakes are especially green in color, they're sometimes called Mojave greens.

Size: These are heavy-bodied, medium-sized snakes, usually about 1½ to 3 feet long; the longest one on record was 4 feet, 3 inches long.

Description: This snake's background color may be greenish gray, olive brown, yellowish green, or brown. The blotches on the back are diamond-shaped or oval to hexagonal and dark gray or brown with light borders; they fade out toward the tail. The tail itself is ringed with light gray and black; the light rings are noticeably wider than the dark rings. On the head, a dark stripe with a light border runs from the eye down to the corner of the mouth. Also on top of the head, between the eyes, a few of the scales are extra large.

Look-alike species: The western diamondback rattlesnake looks similar, but the black and white bands on its tail are equal in width; it also lacks the enlarged scales on the head.

Distribution: In the United States, the Mojave rattlesnake is found in two areas. One region includes the Mojave Desert (southeastern California through southern Arizona and parts of Nevada and Utah); another region is the western edge of south Texas. This snake's home range also extends far to the south into central Mexico. It occurs at elevations from sea level to about 8,300 feet.

Habitat: Mostly a snake of deserts and dry grasslands, it can also be found in a variety of other arid habitats, including juniper woodlands, chaparral, and scrublands. You're most likely to spot it around vegetation such as creosote or mesquite, which provide habitats for rodent prey.

Feeding habits: Mojave rattlesnakes mostly take small mammals such as kangaroo rats, pocket mice, white-footed mice, and ground squirrels, but they will also take lizards and other reptiles.

Distinctive behaviors: Mostly nocturnal, on hot days it spends a lot of time in the coolest places it can find, under rocks or in animal burrows. It has a reputation as an unusually aggressive snake, one that will even advance toward you if disturbed (experts say this reputation is probably an exaggeration, however; but it's best to play it safe, since the Mojave rattler's venom is very potent). During the colder months, Mojave rattlesnakes may hibernate alone or in small groups.

Breeding habits: Not much is known about this snake's reproductive habits. Most young are born in August. Litters can contain two to thirteen offspring; about eight is typical. Newborn snakes are about 10$\frac{1}{2}$ inches long and look like mini adults.

Tiger Rattlesnake
(Crotalus tigris)

Viper Family
(Viperidae)

About the name: *Tigris* is Latin for "of a tiger" and refers to this species' striped back.

Size: A small- to medium-sized snake. Typical adults are about 2 feet long. The biggest specimens are barely 3 feet long.

Description: The background color can vary from individual to individual within a local population, but most snakes are either blue-gray or orange-brown. The tiger-stripe crossbands are somewhat irregular and usually dark gray, olive-green, or brown in color. The tail rings are blurry and indistinct. The head, which has a dark eyestripe, is very small in proportion to the rest of the body; the rattle, however, looks disproportionately large.

Look-alike species: The speckled rattlesnake is similar, but the tiger's unusually small head and lack of tail banding are distinctive.

Distribution: In the United States, this species is restricted to the Sonoran Desert of south-central Arizona, at elevations from one thousand to five thousand feet. Its range extends south into Mexico.

Habitat: This is another snake that manages to make a living in rocky sites in desert habitat. Look for it on rocky mountain slopes, or in rocky canyons and ravines—never on the flats—in desert or grasslands where the vegetation includes mesquite, creosote, cacti, ocotillo, or paloverde.

Feeding habits: Because it has such a small head, some experts think the tiger rattlesnake's diet is mostly restricted to small lizards. Others have reported that it takes a variety of small mammals including kangaroo rats, pocket mice, deer mice, and pocket gophers. The young probably take more lizards than adults do.

Distinctive behaviors: Little is known about this snake's behavior since it's both secretive and little studied. It seems to be most active just after rainstorms; the peak of activity comes with the summer monsoons. It hunts mostly at night, especially during the hot summer months

Breeding habits: Mating season seems to be in the spring. Females bear up to six live young during the summer rainy season. A typical litter is four to six young that average 9 inches long.

Western Rattlesnake
(Crotalus viridis)

Viper Family
(Viperidae)

About the name: The species name, *viridis,* is Latin for "green." The taxonomist who assigned the name probably picked it because, in the Great Plains population, some adult snakes are light greenish-gray in color.

Size: A large snake, with adults often reaching 4 feet long; 5-footers are not unheard of.

Description: Of all the rattlesnakes in North America, this one is the most variable in appearance—there are nine different subspecies. Most individuals have a background color of greenish gray or greenish brown, but this can vary. The subspecies called the Grand Canyon rattlesnake, for example, is a striking salmon pink. Whatever the background color, the back is marked by a string of irregular dark blotches that flatten out into a series of crossbands (like rings) toward the tail. Additional markings include two rows of similar small blotches down each side. The head is very large and wide, offset from the body by a narrow neck. On each side of the face, light stripes run from the front corner of the eye backward to the corner of the mouth. Males are usually longer and heavier than females.

Look-alike species: A number of other rattlesnake species found in the same region may look somewhat similar to this species, but check the tail: Timber rattlesnakes and blacktail rattlesnakes have solid black tails, while Mojave rattlesnakes and western diamondbacks have black-and-white "coontails." In contrast, the bands on a western rattlesnake's tail will always match the colors on its body.

Distribution: In terms of total numbers of square miles, this is the most widely distributed of any rattlesnake in the United States. Draw a line from the Dakotas to Texas: western rattlesnakes live in all the states west of this line. There are also a few populations in northern Mexico and southwestern Canada.

Habitat: Lives in a variety of habitats: prairie grasslands, forests, scrublands, the edges of deserts, even coastal sand dunes. All of these are dry habitats with sparse plant life. The one thing a western rattlesnake needs in all of these places is a place to hibernate that's within reasonable slithering distance, such as a rocky outcrop or the underground burrows of a prairie dog town.

Feeding habits: Takes small mammals such as mice, young prairie dogs, and cottontail rabbits, but also ground-nesting birds such as meadowlarks and their eggs, along with lizards, other snakes, and the occasional frog.

Distinctive behaviors: The western is not known as an aggressive snake; it will glide away rather than rattle and hiss. In warm climates, western rattlesnakes are active year-round and mostly nocturnal; in cooler climates, they forage by day and hibernate during the winter months. Animal burrows, desert tortoise burrows, and prairie dog towns are favorite hangouts, but they will also den in caves, rock crevices, and the walls of wells—anywhere that's below the frost line. They don't mind sharing winter quarters with other rattlesnakes, nonvenomous snakes, and other animals (potential roommates include foxes, badgers, prairie dogs, and burrowing owls). Studies show snakes that huddle together while hibernating lose less water over the course of the winter, which increases their chances of survival.

Breeding habits: Western rattlesnakes are sexually mature after three years in warm climates but take longer to be ready to breed in the far north, where summer hunting seasons are short (up to seven years in British Columbia, for example). Males engage in ritual combat for females. In areas where females are scarce, males spend more time searching and less time fighting. Mating season is between March and May—or snakes may mate in the fall, with females storing sperm over the winter. In later summer to early fall, the female gives birth to four to twenty-one live young (a typical litter is six to eleven, depending on location) that may be 8 to 12 inches long. Larger, older females tend to have more young than smaller, younger mothers.

Ridge-nosed Rattlesnake
(Crotalus willardi)

Viper Family
(Viperidae)

About the name: Taxonomist Seth E. Meek named this species for professor Frank C. Willard (1874–1930), a schoolteacher who discovered the first official specimen in Tombstone, Arizona, in 1905. As for why it's the "ridge-nosed," it really does have ridges along the sides of its nose.

Size: A small snake, with adults measuring just 1 to 2 feet long and weighing only 3 or 4 ounces.

Description: The five subspecies vary in appearance, but the background color is generally brown (gray-brown to reddish brown to dark brown), with narrow crossbands that are white or at least pale in color. Each side is dotted with three rows of small, dark spots. The white stripes on the dark face are distinctive (some historians speculate that the Chiricahua Apaches, whose war paint was a slash of white paint across the cheeks, were specifically imitating this snake). The ridges on each side of the nose (formed by upturned scales) give this snake its name.

Look-alike species: No other snake really looks quite like this. The white facial stripes and ridegenose are distinctive.

Distribution: In the United States, the ridge-nosed rattlesnake can be found in just a few locations in southern Arizona and southwestern New Mexico. It has a wider distribution to the south in northern and extreme southwestern Mexico. This species has been regarded as exclusively a mountain dweller, found at elevations from 5,500 to 9,000 feet, but recently, collectors have reported finding snakes at lower elevations.

Habitat: Each subspecies is found on the slopes of one (or several) mountain ranges. Typical habitat is steep, rocky canyons where pine-oak or conifer forests grow. Look for the snake on rocky outcrops, tucked into crevices where its muted colors blend with the leaf litter.

Feeding habits: Takes a variety of prey, mostly lizards but also centipedes, other small snakes, small mice, songbirds, and scorpions.

Distinctive behaviors: A good climber that sometimes scales high boulders to bask in the sun.

Breeding habits: Mating takes place midsummer to early fall; females store sperm over the winter. Young are born in late July to early August. A typical litter is four to six young. They measure 6 to 8 inches and weigh about $1/2$ ounce—about as much as a quarter.

6

Venomous Snakes in Religion and Culture

Throughout human history, people have made snakes a part of their religious rituals. Sometimes the symbolic serpent is simply a serpent. The snake that tempted Eve in the garden of Eden used venomous words but had no deadly bite. The preeminent god of the Aztecs, the plumed serpent Quetzalcoatl, had showy green feathers and long, dragonlike wings but no venom in its fangs.

In the vast pantheon of heavenly gods and goddesses, however, those that took the form of, or associated with, venomous snakes have always commanded particular awe. After all, how many creatures on earth can deliver death in one quick bite? In this chapter, we'll look at the role that venomous snakes have played in religions and cultures around the world.

Ancient Greece and Rome

Snakes figure prominently in Greek mythology. But though they may be large in size, unusual in shape, terribly ferocious, or all three (Hydra, the snake that Hercules killed for his second labor, had seven heads), the snakes of myth are for the most part nonvenomous.

There are a few exceptions. The dread Medusa and her Gorgons were said to have hair made of venomous snakes. These women looked so hideous that anyone who gazed on them would be turned to stone. A venomous snake also figures in the tragic story of the young lovers Orpheus and Eurydice. Shortly after they are married, Eurydice is pursued by another man. As she runs away to protect her honor, she's bitten by a venomous snake, dies, and is dragged down to Hades. Orpheus, a musician, is heartbroken, and he goes after her. He plays so beautifully on his lyre that the gates of Hell open for him—although in the end, the rescue fails.

The terrifying dog that guards Hades' gates—the three-headed hound Cerberus—was said to have a venomous snake for a tail. Cerberus also had clusters of snakes forming a kind of mane, although these seem to have been the nonvenomous kind.

In ancient Rome, real live venomous snakes were actually used as weapons in a war. The Phoenecian general Hannibal (247–183 BC), an enemy of the Romans and still known today as one of the top military commanders of all time, is credited with inventing biological warfare. Hannibal had the brilliant idea of intimidating his enemies by hurling pots full of venomous snakes at their ships.

Hannibal may be most famous for invading Italy by marching troops mounted on elephants over the Pyrenees. But his unconventional triumph in 190 BC over Rome's ally King Eumenes II of Pergamum was his one and only naval victory. Raining snakes onto the decks of his opponent's fleet, he forced the flustered sailors to fight a battle on two fronts. The distracted men were soon overpowered. The identity of the snakes used in that attack is lost, but a common venomous snake in that region would have been the horned viper, a large grey snake with a black zigzag down its back.

Pliny the Elder was a Roman naval commander who lived in the first century AD. He was also known as a natural philosopher. In his famous *Naturalis Historia,* an encyclopedia of the natural world, he included a most unusual creature called the basilisk, described as a small snake that not only has a venomous bite, but a deadly gaze. Pliny called the basilisk "king of the serpents," in part because it was so lethal, in part because it had a white spot on its head that looked like a crown.

Over time, subsequent readers and translators added extra characteristics and qualities to the basilisk. In the Middle Ages, it was sometimes depicted in illuminated manuscripts and often showed up as an ornamental detail in church architecture. In contrast to Pliny's "small serpent," the later basilisks combined the traits of a snake and a chicken. They had the head, body, and legs of a cock, wings covered with scales, and the tail of a snake. People believed a basilisk was created when a young rooster incubated a serpent's egg.

According to the folk wisdom of the day, if you were going to hunt a basilisk, you had better take along a mirror. That way you could avoid looking at the monster directly—and you could reflect the evil gaze back on the owner, killing it with its own weapon.

Although there really is no such snake as a basilisk, some scientists speculate that Pliny based his description on stories he had heard about venomous cobras in Africa. The Egyptian cobra, for example, has a conspicuous white mark on its head. Other cobra species can "spit" venom—they spray it out under high pressure through tiny holes in their fangs. These snakes don't have to bite you to scare you off: they can look into your eyes and spray venom in them.

Egypt

Each of the gods and goddesses of ancient Egypt was identified with a different animal, and the venomous cobra was sacred to the goddess Wadjet (also know as Uadjet, Edjo, and Uto), whose name means "the green one." In paintings and sculptures, Wadjet was usually depicted as a cobra or as having the head of a cobra. Wadjet's sister, Nekhbet, was the vulture goddess. Together, the two were known as the Nebti. They divided up the kingdom—Wadjet represented Lower Egypt while Nekbet represented Upper Egypt—and symbolized the cycles of life and death. The two sisters would collaborate to crown whomever happened to be king of Egypt. Wadjet, the cobra, was the king's protector; she would spit out venom against his enemies. Pharaohs wearing a stylized golden cobra around their head, called an *uraeus,* are invoking Wadjet.

There were other Egyptian cobra goddesses. Renenutet, depicted as a cobra with a woman's head or as a winged cobra, was a fertility goddess. She was sometimes shown nursing children but was also considered a protector of pharaoh. Another cobra goddess was Meretseger, "she who loves silence," who could punish criminals with blindness. Meretseger was a local goddess who protected the necropolis at Thebes in Upper Egypt. Like Wadjet and Renenutet, she was often depicted as a serpent with a woman's face or simply as a coiled cobra. Ancient Egyptians often put Meretseger figurines into tombs to protect against robbers.

Africa and Asia

Python worship was once a common practice among many native African peoples. But venomous snakes were not regarded with the same reverence as pythons. They were seen as representing the spirits of evil. Because of the slave trade, people from the west coast of Africa brought their religious practices to the Caribbean, where they blended with French and Spanish Catholicism and Native American practices to create the religion today known as voodoo.

Cobras are common in Asia as well as Africa, and the cobra is also an important symbol for those who follow the philosophy of Hinduism. Hindus worship many gods and goddesses, but the fundamental trinity consists of Brahma, Vishnu, and Shiva—the creator, preserver, and destroyer, respectively.

Shiva is associated with the cobra; his job is to destroy all evil and restore the world, and he is usually depicted with a coiled cobra around his neck, symbolizing his power over even the most deadly of creatures. The snake's ability to shed its skin and renew itself symbolizes reincarnation, an important belief in Hinduism, and may also be representative of Shiva's role as one who destroys, then restores. Another reason Shiva can wear a deadly snake around his neck is that he is immortal—he has conquered death. Shiva and the cobra are also associated with fertility.

In the Buddhist tradition, a naga is kind of deity or spirit that may take the form of a hooded cobra with just one head or sometimes with many heads. There are many kinds and forms of nagas, and many stories about them. One well-known naga is Mucalinda, who was said to have sheltered the meditating Buddha from a seven-day downpour with his outspread hood.

The Americas

Snakes, especially rattlesnakes, played an important role in the religious practices of the Aztecs and Mayans. One reason that the Aztecs, whose empire was at its height in central Mexico during the fourteenth, fifteenth, and sixteenth centuries, revered snakes was because they shed their skins whole each year. This natural ability was seen as an expression of the world's endless cycle of rebirth and regeneration, of life emerging from death. Aztec religious rituals that involved the wearing of another human's whole, flayed skin may have been an imitation of the snake's skin-shedding skills.

Aztecs also worshiped snakes because they moved so easily between land and water—they could both slither and swim. In the eyes of the Aztecs, this skill suggested snakes also had the ability to move between the Aztec underworld and the human world.

Aztec temples always featured a variety of beautiful and finely done snake carvings on altars, columns, and walls. Rattlesnakes were most often depicted in these carvings and were considered particularly sacred to Huitzilopochtli, the Aztec god of war.

Rattlesnakes were important to many Native American peoples. The Cherokees, who lived in the Great Smoky Mountains, expressed particular respect mingled with fear for the timber rattlesnakes who shared their landscape. Their names for this species translated to "he has a bell" and "the thunder's necklace."

According to Cherokee tradition, if you dreamed that you had been bitten by a rattlesnake, it was critical that you be treated as if you really had been bitten. Otherwise, you might feel the ill effects of the venom some time in the future, without warning—perhaps years after you'd had the dream.

It was contrary to the Cherokee belief system to kill or even offend a rattlesnake. On rare occasions, a snake might be killed, but only for ceremonial or medical reasons, and only certain specially qualified people had the right to do so. Snake oil was considered to be an especially effective treatment for rheumatism.

Other Native Americans had a different use for other rattlesnake products. The Chiricahua Apache of Arizona, the Blackfoot of northern Montana and Alberta, the Cheyennes of the Plains, and the Maidu of northwest central California all were known to poison the tips of their arrows with rattlesnake venom.

Rattlesnakes are still important today to the Hopi people of northern Arizona. The Hopi are farmers. They grow corn, wheat, and a variety of other crops, including beans, squash, and melons. They also maintain fruit orchards. They live in pueblos on a high plateau, where the climate is dry and rain is critical. So each year, in late August, the Hopi use rattlesnakes in a late-summer religious ritual that's intended to bring rain.

The first step involves catching rattlesnakes of the race of Western rattlesnake called the Hopi rattlesnake. Young men bring the snakes into a kiva, a ceremonial underground chamber, for a purification ritual. On the last day of the ceremony, snake priests perform an elaborate dance. They wear spectacular jeweled and feathered costumes and body paint, and each one dances while holding a snake between his teeth. Another priest dances nearby with an eagle feather, which he uses to distract the snake. At the end of the ceremony, the snake priests grab the snakes in their hands, run into the desert, and release them. The Hopi believe the snakes will carry their prayers for rain to the spirits of the underworld.

Biologists who study snake behavior know snakes tend to hole up in dry weather but come out and forage actively after a rainstorm. It's interesting to speculate whether observations of that activity pattern are what led to this religious ritual.

Snakes in Church

Perhaps it seems strange to learn that even today Hopi priests dance with rattlesnakes clenched in their teeth. But the Hopi are not the only Americans who currently use venomous snakes in worship services. In the eastern United States, some fundamentalist churches routinely use rattlesnakes, cottonmouths, and copperheads as part of their rituals. For them, snake handling is a test of personal faith and Christian obedience.

Snake handlers are members of the "Signs Following" movement, also known as the Church of God with Signs Following. The name comes from Mark 16:19–20: "So then after the Lord has spoken unto them [Jesus's disciples], he was received up into heaven, and sat on the right hand of God. And they went forth, and preached everywhere, the Lord working with them, and confirming the word with signs following." These fundamentalist congregations are part of the Pentecostal Holiness movement that use the King James version of the Bible and interpret scripture literally.

The man who is credited with making the handling of venomous snakes popular in America is George Went Hensley, who was born in 1880 in Tennessee and for a while made his living as a bootlegger. Although illiterate, he became a preacher, and one Sunday morning in 1906 was preaching a sermon at the Church of God in Cleveland, Tennessee, on the Gospel of Mark, Chapter 16:17–18. This text lists the five signs that identify true believers, and one of them is "the taking up of serpents"—literally, a willingness to pick up snakes. The specific text is: "And these signs shall follow them that believe: In my name shall they cast out devils; they shall speak with new tongues; they shall take up serpents; and if they drink any deadly thing it shall not hurt them; they shall lay hands on the sick, and they shall recover." As Hensley was speaking these words, some men dumped a box full of rattlesnakes in front of him. Hensley picked up a large snake and kept preaching.

From there, the practice spread throughout other congregations in the Church of God. Led by the minister, members of the congregation will sing and dance until the atmosphere reaches a fever pitch. Then snakes—usually timber rattlesnakes, but sometimes copperheads and cottonmouths—are hauled from a wooden box and passed around. People drape them around their necks and heads, hold them close to their faces, and kiss and caress them. If someone in the congregation gets bitten, everyone believes it's because either that person has sinned, lacks faith, or is receiving a message from God.

Social scientists who have investigated the phenomenon of snake handling report that most of the people involved are poor whites who are deeply afraid of snakes but feel handling them is a way of expressing their faith and confronting the devil. The snakes used in the ceremonies have not been defanged, milked, or otherwise manipulated in any way, but surprisingly few people have died as a result of snake handling in church: just seventy-seven since the practice started in the 1920s. (One of these was George Went Hensley, killed by an eastern diamondback in 1955.)

In the decades between 1940 and 1950, six southern states banned snake handling as a part of religious rituals: Kentucky, Georgia, Tennessee, Virginia, North Carolina, and Alabama. Today, in the East, only West Virginia allows snake-handling services. In Georgia, although it's a misdemeanor to handle snakes without a permit, the law is loosely enforced, and it's thought that services continue to be held. States west of the Rocky Mountains have no laws governing snake-handling. As of 1996, an estimated two thousand worshipers were thought to still attend snake-handling services.

RESOURCES

Reference Books

Coral Snakes of the Americas: Biology, Identification, and Venoms, by Janis A. Roze. Melbourne, FL: Krieger Publishing Company, 1996.

A scholarly monograph on the New World coral snakes, with keys for identification of all the species and subspecies, as well as distribution maps, information on morphology and anatomy, biology and evolution, even folklore. Special reference to mimicry and cannibalism. Includes a section on snakebite and first aid.

The Encyclopedia of Snakes, by Chris Mattison. New York: Checkmark Books, 1995.

Not really an encyclopedia but a broad look at snakes in general (rather than collection of species accounts). Mattison, who has years of experience as a snake keeper, looks at snake taxonomy, the snake's life cycle, how snakes feed and defend themselves, and even their relationship with humans. Lots of color photographs; appropriate for both scientists and general readers.

Living Snakes of the World, In Color, by John M. Mehrtens. New York: Sterling Publishing Co., Inc., 1987.

This book is notable for documenting, with striking color photographs, more than four hundred of the world's snake species—including a large number of venomous species. Concise information on geographic range, natural history, size, reproduction, and—for hobbyists—care for each species is included. This book was published in 1987, so some of the information has become dated as science moves forward, but enthusiasts know it has a lot of good information between its two covers.

Rattlesnake: Portrait of a Predator, by Manny Rubio. Washington, DC: Smithsonian Institution Press, 1998.

Rubio has combed the scientific literature for an exhaustive look at the natural history of rattlesnakes (all thirty-two species and eighty-three subspecies), but he also has extensive chapters on rattlesnake roundups, conservation issues, and the various ways rattlesnakes and humans have interacted throughout history. The photographs of seldom-seen behaviors are amazing and exceptional.

Snakes of the Southeast, by Whit Gibbons and Mike Dorcas. Athens, GA: University of Georgia Press, 2005.

Dorcas, a Davidson College biology professor, and Gibbons, an ecologist at the Savannah River Ecology Lab, both write about snakes for a popular audience. This comprehensive guide to the fifty-two snake species found in the Southeast is their first collaboration. Heavily illustrated with color photographs and packed with information in an accessible, easy-to-read format, this book answers the questions that people want to know about snakes. Venomous snakes are addressed in a separate section that is well-organized and informative.

Snakes of the United States and Canada, by Carl H. Ernst and Evelyn M. Ernst. Washington, DC: Smithsonian Books: 2003.

Similar in format to *Venomous Reptiles of North America* and also intended as a resource for academicians, this massive reference book has detailed information on all 131 species of snakes found in North America, venomous or otherwise.

Venomous Reptiles of North America, by Carl H. Ernst. Washington, DC: Smithsonian Institution Press, 1992.

Biology professor Carl Ernst is the author of several books about snakes; this one is *the* authoritative monograph on venomous snakes for professional herpetologists in North America. There's a separate entry for each species with a range map and information on geographic distribution, a detailed description, photographs, and information on recognized subspecies, plus information on behavior, reproduction, ecological role, and other technical matters.

Venomous Snakes of the World, by Mark O'Shea. Princeton, NJ: Princeton University Press, 2005.

Most books of this type are organized taxonomically, but O'Shea—curator of reptiles for a safari park in Great Britain and a TV personality in that nation—organizes his subject continent by continent: snakes of Europe, Australia, the Americas, and so on. The book includes detailed species accounts for more than 170 venomous species.

Field Guides

Field Guide to Snakes of North America: Eastern and Central Regions, by Alan Tennant, Richard D. Bartlett, and Gerard T. Salmon. Houston: Gulf Publishing, 2002.

 The companion to the western guide covers snakes from Texas to North Dakota and eastward. Lots of information on subspecies.

Field Guide to Snakes of North America: Western Region, by Richard D. Bartlett. Houston: Gulf Publishing, 1999.

 This guide covers all the species found in western North America, with range maps and information on size, prey, and behavior. Species are depicted with color photographs. Author Richard Bartlett is a herpetologist and herpetoculturalist.

A Field Guide to Venomous Animals and Poisonous Plants: North America North of Mexico, by Roger Caras, Steven Foster, and Roger Tory Peterson. New York: Houghton-Mifflin, 1998.

 Contains useful information on venomous snakes and their look-alikes.

National Audubon Society Field Guide to North American Reptiles and Amphibians. New York: Alfred A. Knopf, 1996.

 This guide is not the most up-to-date as far as taxonomic information is concerned; the range maps are small and lack detail; and subspecies information is not provided. The photos are striking, however, and beginners find this guide easy to use.

U.S. Guide to Venomous Snakes and Their Mimics, by Scott Shupe. Accokeek, MD: Stoeger Books, 2005.

 This guide takes a unique approach, covering not just the venomous snakes of the United States but also their nonvenomous look-alikes. The book includes range maps, full-color photos, and species accounts.

Other Books

Goddess in the Grass: Serpentine Mythology and the Great Goddess, by Linda Foubister. Victoria, BC: EcceNova Editions, 2003.

 From 29,000 BC to the present day, a look at serpent mythology in religions around the world.

Handbook of Clinical Toxicology of Animal Venoms and Poisons, by Jurg Meier and Julian White. Boca Raton, FL: CRC Press, 1995.

 The first concise, one-volume book devoted to the subject. All aspects of the topic are covered including information on the biology and taxonomy of poisonous animals, their venom or poison, diagnosis, and general treatment principles and specific treatment. The most up-to-date list of available antivenins is provided. The editors are internationally recognized authorities in the biology and clinical aspects of venomous and poisonous animals, and the chapter authors are world leaders in their respective fields of toxicology.

Overcoming Animal and Insect Phobias: How to Conquer Fear of Dogs, Snakes, Rodents, Bees, Spiders and More, by Martin M. Antony and Randi E. McCabe. Oakland: New Harbinger Publications, 2005.
> Extreme phobias can detract from the quality of life. This book details research-tested self-help treatments for animal phobias—including the fear of snakes.

Rattlesnake Adventures: Hunting with the Oldtimers, by John W. Kemnitzer, Jr. Melbourne, FL: Krieger Publishing Company, 1996.
> Essays about snake encounters from some well-known herpetologists.

Salvation on Sand Mountain: Snake-Handling and Redemption in Southern Appalachia, by Dennis Covington. New York: Penguin, 1996.
> The author, a freelance Alabama journalist, covered a trial in which a preacher was charged with murdering his wife with rattlesnakes. He went on to attend a snake-handling service, become friendly with the snake-handlers, and ultimately handle snakes himself. This award-winning book is an account of his religious journey and a sympathetic look at the unconventional worship services of a mountain people alienated from the modern world.

The Serpent Handlers: Three Families and Their Faith, by Fred Brown and Jeanne McDonald. Winston-Salem, NC: John F. Blair Publishers, 2000.
> Authors Brown and McDonald, a husband and wife team, derived the information in this book from in-depth taped interviews with three snake-handling families: the Elkinses of West Virginia, the Browns of Tennessee, and the Cootses of Kentucky. The participants were allowed to read and approve the final text so it presents a straightforward account of the lives and beliefs of snake-handling Christians.

The Serpent's Tale: Snakes in Folklore and Literature, by Gregory McNamee. Athens, GA: University of Georgia Press, 2000.
> Snakes in folktales and fairy tales.

Venomous and Poisonous Animals: A Handbook for Biologists, Toxicologists and Toxinologists, Physicians and Pharmacists, by Dietrich Mebs. Pretoria: Medpharm Publications, 2002.
> An introduction to the world of venomous and poisonous animals and how they use their venoms and poisons. Includes first-aid measures and general rules for treating cases of envenoming or poisoning along with recommendations for avoiding dangerous encounters with poisonous animals.

Professional Societies

The following are the preeminent organizations in North America for professional herpetologists.

American Society of Ichthyologists and Herpetologists
Florida International University Biological Sciences
11200 SW 8th St. Miami, FL 33199
www.asih.org

The Herpetologists' League
P.O. Box 519
Bainbridge, GA 39818
www.inhs.uiuc.edu/cbd/HL/HL.html

Society for the Study of Reptiles and Amphibians
Theodora Pinou
Western Connecticut State University
Department of Biological and Environmental Sciences
181 White Street
Danbury, CT 06810
www.ssarherps.org/

Avocational and Societies

Most states have one, or several, herpetological societies or associations. These are regional groups dedicated to the study and appreciation of snakes. Anyone can join these organizations; unlike professional societies; you do not have to have an advanced degree to be a member. Usually, a benefit of membership is that you receive informative publications about snakes. Another benefit is that avocational herpetological societies often bring in interesting and educational speakers.

There are far too many state herpetological organizations to list in these pages. Check the yellow pages or do an online search for the herpetological society in your area (see also "Useful Websites").

Useful Websites

American International Rattlesnake Museum
www.rattlesnakes.com/
The American International Rattlesnake Museum, based in Albuquerque, New Mexico, has the largest collection of different species of live rattlesnakes in the world.

Bell Museum of Natural History
www.bellmuseum.org/herpetology/Links.html
   Check the website of the Minnesota Herpetological Society for links to the websites of many other state herpetological societies.

Center for North American Herpetology
www.cnah.org
   Has extensive links to local, state, regional, and national herpetological society websites.

EMBL Reptile Database
www.embl-heidelberg.de
   A massive database with up-to-date information on the scientific classification of all living reptiles.

National Library of Medicine
www.nlm.nih.gov/medlineplus/ency/article/000031.htm
   Information on the treatment of snakebites.

Scientific and Common Names of the Reptiles and Amphibians of North America—Explained
www.ebeltz.net/herps/etymain.html
   Explains what the scientific and common names of North American reptiles mean.

SPECIES ACCOUNT INDEX